HOW TO STOP OVERTHINKING

THE 7-STEP PLAN TO CONTROL AND
ELIMINATE NEGATIVE THOUGHTS,
DECLUTTER YOUR MIND, AND START
THINKING POSITIVELY IN 5 MINUTES OR LESS

CHASE HILL

SCOTT SHARP

CONTENTS

INTRODUCTION

This book introduces and discusses ways to overcome your overactive mind. That mental chatter or noise your brain produces at night, in the morning, and throughout your day can make it quite difficult to live your life peacefully. Negative thinking, overthinking, and excessive worrying is what makes most people depressed and even anxious. This book touches upon the reasons why you find yourself diagnosed with a "disorder" that you never asked for, as well as how to cope and live with it. There are many techniques that speak about the individual aspects of mental chatter and how to overcome them little by little.

Do you find yourself lying awake at night because you can't stop worrying about what happened earlier that day? Do you find yourself second-guessing almost every decision you face in life? Does your job or friendships seem to be over-whelming? By reading this book, you will be emboldened to deal with your fears, handle your perfectionism, and over-come your diagnosed disorders. One thing you can take away from reading this book is that your thoughts do not define your actions. What you should expect throughout the journey of practicing the techniques and strategies in this book is to be aware of where your mental chatter comes from, and how to address it.

Stop worrying about what you did today and start living in the moment. Stop living for tomorrow and start breathing in the positivity of today. Stop overthinking your future and make big changes to live your future now. We are only ever promised today, so instead of obsessing over what you could have done at that social event or trying to control what you will do in your next appointment, learn to breathe in this moment you have now.

Perhaps the greatest lesson you can learn from reading this book is the simple fact that your thoughts determine the outcome of your life. Even though this may be a difficult statement to swallow (especially for those of you who are now more in your head than you were before), all you need to do in this moment is learn positivity. This book will go through the reasons why the way you think now is not bene-ficial to your being, as well as how positivity can greatly improve and produce where you want your life to go. So, quit being stuck, stop letting your mind trap you, and take control of what you want. There are finally lessons and a structure to get you to where you want to be rather than where you are now. And, it's all in this book.

STEP 1: IDENTIFY YOUR ENEMY AND REASONS FOR OVERTHINKING

Overthinking is when you cannot seem to get something off your mind, and you have uncontrollable or intrusive thoughts that don't seem to go away. It is when you catastrophize everything around you or you are unable to think clearly due to the obsessive amount of thoughts overloading your mind. To overthink means you are focusing on what could be, what should have happened, or the "what ifs" in almost every situation.

Your mind has you trapped in vicious thought-cycles or thought-patterns when you overthink. It's as if you feel mentally exhausted 24/7 due to your brain not being able to unwind or shut down. It is easy to be trapped inside your mind as the world and universe we live in requires us to think about everything we do, everything we want, and everything we believe. Overthinking leads to stress, anxiety, depression, and other mood disorders. Over-thinkers constantly stress about their responsibilities, if they are good people, if they are making the right choices, and whether or not they are productive or unproductive. Thoughts make up who we are or who we want to be as individuals because thoughts lead to actions, and actions lead to character. Since there is so much to think about daily, it is no wonder our brain is on overdrive.

Do you know whether or not you overthink? Maybe you think you do, but then second-guess and convince yourself that you don't which then leads you to ask your original question again later. "Do I overthink everything?" For some people, overthinking is just the way life is for them, and they cannot help but stress about everything. Once you start overthinking, it is challenging to control or even stop it.

Here are some signs your mind has you trapped and is stuck on overdrive:

1. Insomnia

Insomnia develops when people are unable to turn their thoughts off. You may be tired all day, but then when you lay down to sleep or rest, you are instantly awake. Your thoughts flood your mind with everything you haven't done yet, what you want to do, or maybe you didn't perfect something you already did. Your mind obsesses about things you cannot control or things you could have controlled but didn't. This is when you find yourself trapped inside a mental prison. This is also called overthinking, which results in the development of insomnia.

2. Living anxiously

If you cannot relax until you have thought about and planned every scenario for what's to come or what hasn't happened yet, then this is a sign that you are trapped inside your own head. Most people who cannot stop overthinking turn to drugs, alcohol, or prescribed medication to drown out their thoughts just to get some peace. If your thoughts are causing you to be anxious and you fear the unknown and seem to need control, then this is a sign you are living in fear and have fallen into a trapped mind.

3. Overanalyzing everything around you

Much like what was said for the previous symptom, the need to control is overwhelming and is one of the main problems consisting of overthinking habits. The need to control every-thing means that you try to plan the future, which is unknown, so you fear failure and obsess over what you are doing now to stop bad things from happening. You are not living in the moment, which gives you a significant amount of anxiety because your mind is busy with everything else. Someone who over-analyzes things has a hard time accepting change because change is rarely planned, which sends them in a downward spiral as now they are facing something they do not have power over. Due to this habit, overthinking leads to poor decision-making skills because of the indecisiveness of what to do next.

4. Fear of failure (aka Perfectionism)

Perfectionists also like to control things; however, they control projects and their surroundings, making sure they get everything right in fear of making a mistake. Perfection-ists cannot accept failure and go to great lengths to avoid it. As a result of this type of behavior, perfectionists will stray away from making big decisions or accepting big opportuni-ties because they would rather not do anything over taking the risk that they could fail.

5. Second-guessing yourself

Stemming from the overwhelming fear of failure and perfectionism, the mind of a "control freak" will often analyze, reanalyze, second-guess, then come up with another analyzation, to the point where nothing seems good enough, so this loop repeats itself. Someone who cannot accept change or does not believe in themselves fully will second-guess out of the fear of making the wrong move or decision. Also, they take twice as long to process information because they second-guess other people and question if they interpreted the conversation right or not. If this happens to you, then consider yourself an over-thinker.

6. Headaches

In the result of second-guessing and thinking about things over and over again, headaches start happening because the mind cannot seem to get any peace for even a minute. Headaches are a sign we need to take a break and unwind or settle down. It is a sign that we need to cope or find strategies to relax our minds and our bodies. Headaches also stem from body tension, which is a sign of stress.

7. Sore muscles and stiff joints

Overthinking is one of the number one causes of stress. When you continue to overthink, your brain connects this to the way things should be and, as a result, traps you. This leads to overwhelming and negative thought-patterns, obsessive worrying, anxiety, OCD, and other mood or stress-related disorders. When someone is overly stressed or thinks way too much, it affects their entire body. Only when you find and solve the root of your stressors or problems will the pain and aches disappear. Once your brain attacks your body and muscles, your emotions and mood become affected as well, which can leave you feeling exhausted and mentally drained or fatigued.

8. Fatigue

As explained in the last symptom, we will feel fatigued if we take on too much for our body and minds to handle. Fatigue is your body's way of telling you that you are about to burn out. If you are on the go all the time, not just physically but mentally as well, then burnouts are bound to happen. It's like an electronic device that needs batteries, if it is left on 24/7 or continues to play without being charged, then it will die or need its batteries replaced. Fatigue is the brain's way of letting you know that it requires a reboot or that you need to rest or else you will run out of energy.

9. Cannot be present

Do you find yourself trying to listen to others talk, but your mind distracts you with your own thoughts? Or, do you find yourself trying to be in the moment with your kids or spouse, yet are too busy obsessing over what you need, what needs to be done, or what has been forgotten (because there has to be something)? This means that your mind has you trapped in the wonderful world of overthinking. Isn't it great? Not… Thinking too much can cause you to lose focus or sight of the most important things in life. Remember to slow down, as not everything needs to be rushed. After all, you still have more life to live and lead.

As you can see, these symptoms or signs that you are an over-thinker relate to one another. For example, you start by overanalyzing and second-guessing things, which stems from the fear of failing, which gives you anxiety because of the lack of control for the unknown future. When this happens, headaches and stiff muscles develop which then leads to a lack of sleep, resulting in insomnia and fatigue, which then complicates things to let you be able to stay in the present moment. Overthinking and obsessive worrying is hard to control, but there is some light. By the end of this book, you will develop and know exactly what to change and how to change it without being fearful of the consequences. Think of this book, as you read on, as your comprehensive guide to getting better and leaving those pesky thoughts in the dust.

Stop Overthinking

If there were such a thing or ability to stop your thoughts, then wouldn't you jump on the opportunity? Imagine you being able to get more rest and quiet your mind to find peace. This is possible; however, you must develop patience, drive, motivation, and resilience. I will discuss more on the techniques of how to stop overthinking and worrying for good in the coming chapters, but for now, let's briefly focus on how to stop overthinking.

The reason you need to be patient is that not everyone becomes a master at calming their thoughts overnight, so resilience is needed because you need to be aware that you could possibly fail, but practice makes things easier. Every day that you practice quieting the mind is one step closer to the advantages of having inner peace and living mindfully. Also, later we will discuss why it is so important to be motivated and to address your overthinking patterns.

It is completely normal to overthink once in a while, but when it becomes a pattern that eventually unfolds and continues to disrupt your everyday life, then that is when it has become a problem. Two thought patterns involve destructive overthinking:

• Ruminating - Rehashing the past

Ruminating thoughts consists of overthinking things that you cannot control or things that have happened that you obsess over. For example, say you went to a meeting and stated your opinion on a certain topic, later you tell yourself you shouldn't have done that, then you obsess over what you could have said differently. Also, negative thinking stems from ruminating thoughts, such as thinking about what someone said that was negative about you, and then you believe it because of something that you did prior to this thought. For example, you remember your friends or peers telling you that you wouldn't go far, and now you are starting to believe it.

• Excessive worrying - Predicting the future negatively

You may sit there and tell yourself that you aren't going to do a good job in your presentation tomorrow. Or, you may sit there and think that you aren't good enough, so your spouse or partner may find someone else. You don't believe in yourself, so you aren't confident in how things will turn out because you are fearful of your future, which is unknown.

Over-thinkers imagine the worst-case scenarios and get anxious based on these "visions." It is one thing to think negatively and worry or ruminate about negative outcomes or experiences, and it is another problem when images or photographic images play in your mind. For example, imagine you are going to grab your kids from school; you have five minutes to spare before they are outside waiting for you. On the way to their school, your car breaks down, and now you have to call for help. Your mind shows you an image or "vision" that your kids are waiting, no one is there to grab them, and then some stranger comes to pick them up, and now your kids are gone. You then start feeling anxious, and your mind plays tricks on you to make you believe you are a bad parent or caregiver. This is the mind trap of what overthinking does. When this happens, stop and take a moment to reflect and not only call for help, but also call the school and let the principal know what has happened, then make another call for someone else to grab your children. When you take a moment to reflect and think about the best-case scenario, your mind doesn't have time to stress over what is irrational and is most likely not going to happen.

Studies[1] suggest that overthinking leads to mental health issues and less sleep, which then leads to alcohol or drug use as a way to cope. So, let's dive in to figure out how to put an end to this ruminating, over-worrying nightmare. Practice these strategies for some peace and quiet up there, and more restful nights:

1. Notice when you are overthinking.

Practice self-awareness. When you do this, you can be aware of when those pesky thoughts creep in. Being aware of your triggers and what the first sign of being trapped in the overthinking habit is are the first steps to escaping the cycle. When you notice yourself obsessing over things you cannot control or stressing about the past, acknowledge them and notice that they are there without getting anxious or being judgmental. Tell yourself that you are going to allow ten minutes to think about whatever is worrying you. Set a timer. Realize that thinking this way isn't productive as it isn't going to change anything, and then move on to what else is worrying you. Once you've completed this process, do some deep breathing and distract yourself with something else.

2. Challenge your thoughts.

Challenging your thoughts is a productive way to get out of the negative, overthinking pattern that your mind wants you to stay in. If you find yourself thinking that, because you are late, you are going to get fired, or you will be late on rent so you will be homeless, then take a step back. Notice that you are worrying about things that haven't happened yet and think about the best-case scenario. If you can't help but think about the worst-case scenario, then first think about how not to let the worst case happen. For example, if your alarm didn't go off and you are going to be late for work, then instead of listening to your thoughts and running around in a frenzy, challenge your thoughts. Ask yourself what you can do. Can you call into work and let them know you're running late? Can you make it on time? What can you do to avoid this from happening again? Is it worth stressing over this to be perfect? Realize and understand that no one is perfect. When you take a step back to think about things logically, you will see that things get done faster and easier.

3. Focus on problem-solving.

Much like challenging your thoughts, work on ways you can solve problems. Why dwell on problems when you can solve them? Don't ask yourself **why** something happened; rather, ask yourself **what** you can do about it. When you make steps and think of solutions to your problems and stressors, you teach your brain that you are in control and it rewires itself to automatically solve problems effectively the more you practice. So take more moments to slow down and acknowledge the problem, instead of breaking it and yourself apart. Look for solutions and ask yourself **how** you can change it. If it cannot be changed, then let it go and focus on something else.

4. Practice and research mindfulness.

Mindfulness is an excellent technique that can help anyone in the moment. Being mindful is to stay present in the moment you are in. It suggests that nothing else matters except for this time, this place, and this being. It is to be one with yourself and your thoughts. Think about it: How can you focus on the past or the future if you are intentionally paying your full attention to the here and now? With practice, mindfulness is a great technique for reducing over-thinking and negative thoughts.

5. Change the channel.

If I told you to **not** think about a purple elephant jumping on pink clouds, then what are you going to do? No matter how hard you try, you are going to think about the color of the elephant and what it is doing. The same goes for when you try to stop doing something. So when you tell yourself not to think about something, it is bound to backfire. Instead, acknowledge your thoughts and distract yourself with something else, like exercise or call a friend to vent and listen to them vent. When you focus on other people or other things, you are more likely to spend your time doing something different than overthinking and worrying. Another productive idea is to get creative. Draw a picture that symbolizes your thoughts, write a journal entry, or rhyme your current mood with other words. Play a scrabble game or interact with things around the house. Sometimes all it takes is just to get out of the house, go outside, or remove yourself from where you are currently. This is also a strategy to "reboot" your overactive mind. We will talk more about this later.

In conclusion, the more you practice these techniques, the better you will get at quieting your mind. When your mind is quiet, you will be able to think things through better.

When you can think things through, you can make effective decisions without having negative thoughts interrupt your efforts. Eventually, over time, your mind will learn how to tune out the unnecessary worries on its own, and you will feel less stressed and be able to handle problems better.

How Deep of an Over-thinker Are You?

Now that we have gone over the signs of overthinking and what you can do to avoid or diminish it, we can focus on how much of an over-thinker you are. Sometimes over-thinking is due to an underlying problem, like generalized anxiety disorder (GAD). GAD involves constant uncontrollable worrying, nervousness, and tension build-up. The reason it is called "generalized" is because you don't fear just a specific thing, but you fear almost everything, as everything makes you anxious due to your excessive thought-patterns. It only becomes a disorder when you can't control it and when it starts to take over your life by giving you situational symptoms or when you have "panic attacks" over your thoughts. The goal of this section is to figure out how much of an over-thinker you are or if it ties into anxiety or another mood disorder.

This is a test you can take online to figure out if you have anxiety and what kind:

http://www.heretohelp.bc.ca/screening/online/?screen=anxiety

This is a test to figure out if you are an over-thinker, and if you are, then how deep. It also has tips and tricks and infor-mation that is crucial to understanding what it means to be an over-thinker:

https://www.happierhuman.com/overthinking/

This is an online test where you can see if depression is the root of your overthinking patterns:

https://www.psycom.net/depression-test/

These tests are not to diagnose yourself, but to gain insight on if you need to speak with a doctor.

Is Overthinking a Disorder?

By now you should already know if you are an over-thinker based on your routines and your life choices. So, the next question is to ask yourself if there is a deeper problem behind it. Overthinking can be the primary cause of an anxiety disorder or depression. This is because when we are stuck in our minds, we continuously worry about things we think we can control but actually cannot. We get depressed when we continue to think negatively and cannot seem to control our thought-patterns revolving around these nega-tive thoughts. Many people ask if overthinking is a disorder, and the answer is yes. Many people also suffer from thinking too much about things, such as if they made the right choice or if they are going down the "right" path. The fact of the matter is that nothing is ever "right" or "wrong," but it's if we set these beliefs inside our own minds and then strive to complete the goals of what is right or wrong. For example, when we meet someone's family for the first time, we may think, *"Did I say the right thing?"* or, *"Did I make the 'right' impression?"* In reality, this person's family isn't even thinking or judging you based on your own judgments. So, in this sense, nothing is "right" or "wrong." When faced with this "right or wrong" attitude or belief, try to focus on the moment and practice mindfulness intentionally.

Overthinking only becomes a disorder when it becomes the only thing you do, and it interrupts your daily needs. When you cannot get things done or are fearful of making mistakes, overthinking becomes a disorder, which then brings on anxiety, depression, and other mood disorders. However, if you are just worried about the same things every day but don't let it affect your decisions, then you don't necessarily have an overthinking disorder. If you always worry about yourself, your life, your health, your family, your friends, and so on, then it also may not be a sign of having an overthinking disorder. If you find yourself worrying about or being too concerned about other's lives and their worries or fears, then it may just suggest you have an empathetic personality. So, how do you know if you have an overthinking disorder? One or more of these symptoms are signs of that you may be a sufferer:

• You compare yourself to others and question their judgments by setting too high expectations for yourself. You are constantly worrying about what others think rather than just being confident in your own skin.

• Catastrophizing every scenario or situation in your life. Thinking or imagining the worst will happen, which results in thinking that everything and everyone is "out to get you."

• Unable to move past your failures or mistakes. Continuously thinking about how you could have done something different or how you should or shouldn't have said or done something, then feeling overwhelming anxiety and nervousness about it.

• Setting "farfetched" goals and thinking that you will never be able to accomplish them. Never setting goals you can actually do, so you feel overwhelmed and don't do anything to work towards them as a result.

• The inability to shut off your overactive mind, leaving you fatigued and constantly stressed.

If these symptoms seem or feel familiar, then it may be best to see a professional for your mental health and to address your concerns. A professional, like a doctor or therapist, can give you coping methods and other tools to help you with overthinking. If you have these symptoms, then you may also find that you have communication problems due to the inability to listen fully, you may find it difficult to enjoy hobbies or interests, or you may be unproductive at work because of your obsessive, perfectionist traits.

By thinking too much or if you are unable to "unwind," other mood disorders, such as anxiety, GAD, depression, insomnia, and obsessive-compulsive disorder (OCD) can become prominent in your everyday life.

We have now learned what overthinking is about and what it can cause; however, there are other symptoms and causes stemmed from overthinking which we will talk more about as you read through this book. We will discuss in more detail the symptoms of GAD, depression, and OCD in the next chapter because these mood disorders mainly revolve around worrying too much. We will also discuss the things you can do to seek help if you are diagnosed already or have a feeling you may be getting to this point. In the next chapter, I talk about worrying, facing your fears, and will explain in detail what the brain does when you overthink or worry too much.

STEP 2: 10 POWERFUL TACTICS TO STOP ANXIETY AND WORRYING PERMANENTLY

There is worrying, and then there is over-worrying. Much like overthinking, over-worrying is when you torment yourself with thoughts of the past, present, and future and try to control what cannot be controlled. It is a condition where you can feel an overload of stress and anxiety, constantly feeling uneasy, even over small things. Disorders like anxiety, OCD, and depression can be a result when someone develops excessive worrying. We suffer by making it difficult to overcome our fears because we are too scared of the fear itself to problem-solve and come up with a solution. There are differences between over-thinkers and excessive worriers. Worry stems from fear, whereas overthinking stems from denial.

Fear:

Worry brings us self-doubt and constant fear of the unknown, making it difficult to accept and encounter changes in our lives. Fear makes us avoid things we want to do because it traps us in our minds as a way to keep us safe. However, fear is an illusion. When we are fearful of change or the unknown, we miss opportunities that are right in front of us, like a promotion, meeting new people, and potential knowledge to make ourselves better. We will talk more about fear and how to control it later.

Denial:

Most times, we deny what we want, so instead we cling to denial to prevent ourselves from enduring discomfort or painful emotions. To cope with denial or endure more denial from other people, we may use distractions like drugs, alcohol, prescription medication, exercise, or work so that we don't have to face our truth. On the other hand, some people use thoughts, which then leads to overthinking because they cannot or do not want to accept what is or what was.

If you do not get a grasp on your thoughts, causing you to worry excessively, then you will end up with more stress, which is also the leading cause to mental health problems. Luckily, this book will give you insight on how to stop worrying to decrease the chance of disorders forming so that you can live a healthier life.

Mental Health Issues

In the last chapter, we briefly explained what GAD is, so let's talk in more detail about it now. Generalized anxiety disorder, in short, is a disorder where worries and fears take over your life and interrupt healthy habits, making it difficult to develop healthy and effective behaviors. There are people who worry about things in a productive way, such as having a thought, noticing it, thinking about it, and letting it go. The reason why this effect is healthier is because worrying doesn't take over your mind and you are still able to do things you like to do, as you don't have an overwhelming fear of what you can't control. You understand that worrying isn't going to change anything, and it is easy to distract yourself or think of other things, whereas GAD takes on a totally different effect. People with GAD find it very difficult to distract themselves from their worries and intrusive thoughts. They expect the worst in every situation and develop symptoms of an "anxiety attack" as a result of their brain and body being too stressed. GAD sufferers find it extremely difficult to slow down and be in the present moment.

Here are some signs that someone may be suffering from GAD:

Emotional

• Excessive worrying and intrusive thoughts that cannot be slowed down or controlled;

• No matter what someone does, they cannot seem to avoid intrusive or negative thoughts daily;

• Cannot handle uncertainty or change. They need to know, plan, or control what their future holds;

• A sudden feeling of dread or fear when worries take over.

Behavioral

• They are unable to relax, always tense, and cannot enjoy alone time or seem to unwind;

• They have an inability to focus or concentrate on tasks, work, or school;

• Due to feeling overwhelmed by their worries, they procrastinate or cancel events or "to-dos" often;

• Due to anxiety attacks in certain situations, they will avoid going out or entering situations in fear of that they will become overloaded by their thoughts. They may also think too much before the event, so they avoid going or doing anything that triggers their anxiety.

Physical

• Constant muscle pressure or joint stiffness. Body feels tense on a daily basis;

• Due to having an overactive mind, sleepless nights become more dominant and may develop insomnia;

• Feeling constantly on edge or restless, and may scare easily;

• Gut problems such as stomach cramps, nausea, and diarrhea or constipation.

This list of symptoms may seem like a lot, but the plus side is that with the right guidance and help, you can and will find ways to cope. Another disorder that can form due to over-worrying is OCD.

OCD stems from anxiety disorders, but instead of being afraid of your thoughts and worries, it is characterized by having to do things based on what you are thinking. For example, someone who suffers from OCD may wash their hands twenty times a day or count all the red things in a room before they can do anything else. It does not bring any pleasure to the individual, but it is a way for them to handle their own anxieties. OCD is characterized by unwanted intrusive thoughts that make you feel as though you must act repetitively or have ritualized behaviors, such as counting, singing, washing, tapping, moving, or having things arranged a certain way. If these tasks or behaviors are not completed exactly when the person feels they need to do them, then it causes large amounts of panic because they cannot resist the urge to do that specific thing. In short, it is when the brain gets stuck on a particular thought or urge that does not go away until practiced or rehearsed - much like a CD or disk that skips when it is scratched, unable to continue the song. It's as if the person cannot continue their day until they act on this thought or urge that they have.

Signs indicating that you may have OCD are presented below:

Thoughts

• Fear of germs, getting contaminated, or contaminating others;

• Fear of losing control of yourself or your surroundings, resulting in you hurting yourself and/or others;

• Uncontrolled and unwanted, disturbing thoughts revolving around sexual or violent images;

• Exaggerated focus on religious or moral concepts;

• Fear of forgetting something or leaving something behind that you may need;

• Superstitious;

• The idea or thought that everything has its place, and everything must be a certain or specific way.

Behaviors

• Constant rechecking of appliances, locks, clocks, and switches;

• Excessive control over loved one's safety so you continuously check in on them;

• Counting, tapping, repeating words or phrases, or reducing anxiety in other irrational ways;

• Ritually cleaning yourself or your surroundings;

• Arranging things exactly as you NEED to have them in order to not trigger fear and panic;

• Hoarding "junk," such as newspapers, rocks, food containers, clothes, or other things.

Although OCD can be difficult to live with or see someone else struggle with, help can be found. Later, we will discuss ways you can stop or cope with excessive worrying, and these strategies and tips will help with disorders concerning anxiety, depression, and OCD. Speaking of depression, this is another disorder that can stem from over-worrying.

There is sadness, and then there is depression. Depression is more than just a dull or upset mood; it is when our negative thoughts become uncontrollable and we view the world as nothing more than negativity. You develop this way of thinking to the point where it seems impossible to get out of, so we give up trying or caring, which leaves us depressed. It can be difficult to get up in the mornings and you may lose interest in activities you would normally enjoy. Depression disrupts your way of living, attacking important habits like eating, sleeping, working, and studying. Some people describe depression as feeling empty or hopeless, causing one to believe that there is no point to life or that nothing can bring happiness.

The symptoms of depression are as follows:

• Feeling helpless or empty. Overwhelming, black-and-white thinking, such as nothing will get better and there is nothing you can or will do about it;

• Loss of interest in activities you used to enjoy, like sex, hobbies, and socializing. You do not feel joy or pleasure and don't feel the need for these feelings;

• Eating habit changes; You may lose weight due to the lack of interest in eating or gain weight due to "eating your feelings";

• Sleep disturbances. Either not getting enough sleep due to insomnia, or oversleeping due to the hopelessness your brain makes you feel about life;

• Anger and frustration. Your patience level is low, you have a quick fuse, and everything seems to get under your skin;

• Fatigued or drained. Due to the consistent thoughts that

run through your mind daily, you feel tied down and lose energy due to your habits, like your sleep and eating patterns;

• Low self-esteem. You are not confident, and you believe the worst in yourself and in other situations. You are so tired of your unwelcomed negative thoughts that you give up hope and lose motivation to get better;

• Trouble with concentration. You have a hard time focusing on tasks, making decisions, and remembering things due to your overactive mind that continues to weigh you down.

It is easy to confuse depression with bipolar disorder because they both involve similar feelings and symptoms. However, bipolar disorder is when you have high energetic moods and low depressing moods. People with this mental health issue find it difficult to balance their emotions or keep a steady, "neutral" mood. Bipolar disorder can also be confused with personality or derealization disorders.

As you can see, overthinking, which converts to excessive worrying, which then progresses into negative thought-patterns, can have a great effect on your mental health. It is best to seek help from a doctor or psychiatrist if you feel you have any of the symptoms from these disorders above. On the other hand, try not to worry or think too much about whether you have these or not. If you haven't been diag-nosed already or experienced these symptoms prior to reading this book, then you most likely don't need to worry about developing these mental health issues. Continue reading to learn more about what goes on in the brain, and then we can dive into the healthy habits of decreasing constant stress revolving around your worried mind.

What Happens in the Overactive/Worried Brain?

Now that we have some more information about what excessive worrying can cause, let's figure out how our brain works if we develop these disorders or live life worrying on a daily basis. Did you know that your brain actually changes and looks different as a result of the long-term effects of stress? Researchers have examined and compared the brain of a diagnosed depressed individual to an individual who didn't have depression, and the MRI (magnetic resonance imaging) scan showed that the individual who had diagnosed depression had a slightly different brain than the other individual. The MRI, a device used to look inside the brain, showed that people with chronic depression had a smaller hippocampus and a thinner right cortex. The hippocampus part of the brain is responsible for memory, and the right cortex is responsible for our mood.

Because depression primarily revolves around the way we self-talk and view the world based on negativity or positivity, it is fair to say that excessive worrying could be the cause as to why regions in the mind that focus on reward-processing become less active. The reward processors in the brain are responsible for the "feel good" receptors, such as serotonin and dopamine. The "feel good" chemicals excite us about things like hobbies, socialization, and new events. When this part is less active, it can be hard to be excited about these things.

When people are worried for a considerable length of time, their serotonin and dopamine levels decrease, resulting in higher levels of depression and anxiety. If not treated or noticed, it can increase and cause more problems. Let's take a look at what these chemicals do:

Serotonin:

Serotonin regulates mood, emotions, and sleep. This chemical is responsible for making you excited, keeping a positive attitude, and feeling less stressed or worried. If you constantly worry, then your serotonin levels may be lower than normal.

Dopamine:

Dopamine affects subconscious movement, conscious awareness and attention, and pleasurable feelings. When you have sexual intercourse or exercise, high levels of dopamine increase in your brain, which is why you experience a euphoric feeling when you engage in these activities. If your dopamine levels are low, you may find it hard to concentrate or feel the need to participate in "feel good" activities.

Norepinephrine:

This chemical is responsible for feelings of arousal, sleep, attention, and mood. Basically, it combines the two other chemicals and produces more of the "feel good" receptors when we choose to make healthy habits or control our anxious thoughts.

The thing about anxiety that most people don't realize is that our body and soul need anxiety to get us out of dangerous situations, such as if we get involved in a car accident or are running from something. Anxiety brings on the "fight, flight, freeze" response, which is useful for when we are in real danger. These responses activate in our body, giving us the adrenaline we need to do whatever action necessary. When we are in an unsafe environment, chemicals and hormones in our body get triggered which heightens our senses and allows us to fight better, run faster, or stay still and silent longer. The problem with this, though, is that if we develop an anxiety "disorder," our "fight, flight, freeze" response activates with false fears and can come on suddenly or gradually.

So, what happens in the brain that causes these "false alarm" triggers? Did you know that before your body starts feeling symptoms of an anxiety or panic attack, the brain is already forming thoughts, behaviors, and getting ready to provide physical symptoms, before you are even aware? This is why most psychologists or doctors will ask you to pay attention to what you were thinking or doing before the fear developed inside your body. Excessive worrying can trigger an attack, which forms from thought-patterns and daily habits. The amygdala and hippocampus play a substantial role in most "worry warts," resulting in chronic anxiety or continuous stress.

Amygdala:

This part of the brain is responsible for the connection between the areas of the brain that process incoming sensory messages and the areas that understand these signals. It is located deep inside the brain and looks like an almond-shaped structure. This is the part of the brain that triggers alerts or danger. The amygdala has an emotional-memory part stored inside and may be the reason why we are scared of certain things such as sights (dogs, spiders, flying), smells (childhood smells or familiar smells that trigger danger), tastes (food or other tastes that make up paranoia or hypochondria - like if someone was ever poisoned), and sounds (noises, such as storms, banging cupboards, or yelling). With that being said, it is fair to believe post-traumatic stress disorder (PTSD) is a result of an overactive amygdala.

Hippocampus:

Not only is the hippocampus responsible for the memory part of the brain, but it also transmits threatening events. In people with PTSD, child abuse, or a violent or troubled history, their hippocampus is actually smaller than those who were not victims of their past. It is believed that people with smaller hippocampi conjure or create unwanted flash-backs of traumatic memories. These people struggle to put memories in chronological order and suffer from short-term memory loss as a result of a weaker hippocampus.

Norepinephrine and cortisol are your body's natural chemicals that are accountable for boosting your perception, reflexes, and speed in unsafe situations. They also increase your heart rate, pump more blood and oxygen into your muscles and lungs, and get you prepared to face whatever it is you are going to suffer. However, when it is a false alarm, these spikes still take effect, and when you are not facing real danger, these high levels of chemicals and hormones rushing through your body have nowhere to go because they are not being used effectively. As a result, you may instead become paralyzed and end up shaking, sweating, and unable to breathe, among many other physical symptoms. Can you imagine all this just because you overthink or worry excessively over everything? Your body is going through a lot more than you would think when it's just one thought that could trigger an overload of stress-related symptoms. Luckily, there are ways to reduce excessive worrying and create habits that can increase productivity in your life, so you don't fall into this vicious trap.

Effective Skills to Stop Worrying

Let's focus solely on how to get you to stop worrying. Keep in mind though, that in order to cope with or stop worrying entirely, it will take motivation, time, patience, and lots of practice. It will not happen overnight, but there is light at the end of this nightmare IF you stay consistent and dedicated to training your worried and troubled mind.

Regardless of the "scientific" studies or research that consists of what happens in the brain, the more you practice healthy habits to stay away from the negative patterns, the more developed your brain will become, and eventually your mind will make new connections and instinctively handle worry-related situations productively. First, let's discuss cognitive distortions and why they can be hard to get out of your head. Once we understand why we seem to be unable to get out of our worried state, then we can start practicing the techniques with these distortions in mind.

Cognitive distortions[1] are irrational thought-patterns brought on by long-term habits and false beliefs we tell ourselves in order to manage fears or anxieties. However, we need to realize that these beliefs - you may think you are unable to handle something when you really can - are just irrational and unnecessary "security blankets" or "safety nets" we create in our minds to make us feel better. This results in the mental trap of excessive worrying. Here are examples of cognitive distortions:

• All-or-nothing thinking:

This is black-and-white thinking. There is no middle ground or compromise. *Someone said I am a failure, so it must be true.*

• Overgeneralization:

Thinking that one outcome rules every outcome. *I didn't get the job, so I am not good enough and will never get a job.*

• Only thinking negatively, avoiding the positive:

This is when you do not allow yourself to see the positive in a situation and you only focus on the negative aspects. *I must be really dumb because the only question I got wrong was the last one.*

• Making excuses as to why positive circumstances in an event don't matter:

Even though there were positive things that happened, you see them, and you still make excuses for them. *I did really well presenting myself in front of the employer, but they probably just had a good day, so I won't get the job.*

• Making false, negative predictions:

You predict that something in the future, without evidence, will actually happen. *I know for sure something bad is going to happen.*

• Expecting the worst:

You over-exaggerate outcomes or tell yourself something horrible is going to happen. *The train was late. That must mean it broke down and now everything is delayed. I won't be able to make my appointment on time, which means I will get fired.*

• Having beliefs of what "should" and "shouldn't" be:

When you don't follow your own beliefs of what should and shouldn't happen, you beat yourself down. *I should have known that was going to happen. I can't do anything right.*

• Labeling yourself based on your failures:

Because of something you did wrong or you may have disappointed yourself or someone else, you may think: *I don't deserve a second chance because I always do this. I am a disgrace.*

- **Assuming you are responsible for things you cannot control:**

It's my fault that my grandma's vase broke; I should have been watching my son and been more careful.

So, why is it so hard to quit obsessing over your worries? You may not be completely aware that you are thinking through these cognitive distortions. Many people start thinking this way long before results of excessive worrying or "disorders" arise. You believe that worrying will help you solve a problem or prevent you from future events that you were unaware of. However, worrying does not get you anywhere, and the only thing you can do is practice effective skills to stray away from this uncontrollable, negative thinking. To give up worrying is essential because it means you can give up the thought that worrying serves a positive purpose.

How to Stop Worrying for Good

Worrying has been proven to create more restless or sleepless nights, attack your immune system, raise the chances of developing PTSD, and increase the risk of dying at a younger age. The thought behind worrying that causes so much anxiety is that people cannot accept one simple truth: We **do not** have **control** over certain things that happen in our lives. The primary reason most people worry is because they either second-guess every choice or decision they make, or they cannot accept that they don't have control, and so they become perfectionists or "control freaks" to make themselves feel better. However, is the need to control or perfect everything really making you feel better? If your answer is no, then take a look at these ways you **can** control your mind in a **positive** way:

1. Set a "worry time"

By setting a specific time for when you can worry, you practice telling your worries that you don't have time right now, but that you will have some time later to address the problems. Make sure this "worry time" is not right before bed or in the middle of a hectic time of day, like cooking dinner. Make sure it is no longer than an hour. That way, it gives you plenty of time to address all your worries and come up with effective solutions. Also, end your "worry session" with meditation or calm-breathing exercises.

Acknowledge the thought or worry

ASK yourself CAN you fix the worry?

When there is a worry that arises during your day that you cannot let go of, write it down and acknowledge it. Do not try to avoid the thought or push it away, as this will only make it worse and "louder." Accept that the worry may not go anywhere and move on. Don't pay too much attention obsessing over it; just acknowledge that it is there. When you are in your "worry time," look at the notes you wrote throughout the day and assess these first.

Write them down and pick them apart

Keep a journal. This is effective because when we try to think about our worries during a busy day, we are most likely thinking illogically or irrationally. When we write our worries in a journal, we can not only vent, but we can also see the patterns in our thinking to pick the negative thoughts out and replace them with positive ones. It also helps us look at our worries as a whole, so we can gain better insight as to what to do next.

2. Practice mindfulness

Mindfulness is when you intentionally allow yourself to be in the present moment. It's to look at the red colors and count how many things in the room are red (or any other color). If you are drinking or eating something, then it is to be completely present with the taste, texture, smell, and sight of the item you are consuming. So, in a deeper meaning, when a worry arises, don't pick it apart, don't judge it, don't get anxious about it – simply understand that this worry is just a thought and that is all it is. There is no action you need to take; there are no feelings you need to attach to it; there is nothing you need to do with this thought except to be mindful that it is there. If you are having trouble with this, seek professional, therapeutic help or look up videos on the internet to walk you through this process.

3. Exercise/Get physical

Tons of studies from all over and almost everything you

44

read says that mental health disorders may be coming from the gut. When we eat better and healthier things, we have more energy. When we have more energy, we can discover productive ways to release this energy, like working out and exercising. Go for a mindful jog, a relaxing yoga class, or do sit-ups and on-the-spot exercises from the comfort of your own home, like running in place, squats, and push-ups. It may be a good idea to enroll in boxing classes or join a sport. Also, when you get your blood flowing and your heart pumping, you have less energy mentally to focus on the many worries that pop in your head, which also helps you sleep better at night.

4. Figure out what is out of your control

This works best when you have a therapist or guidance counselor to help you, but in case you want to try this on your own for whatever reason, find what you can control and let go of what you can't. For example, you cannot control someone else's behavior, but you can control how you react and what you perceive from their words or actions. Understand that, in most cases, you can only control how you react or behave in situations or when confronting someone else.

5. Evaluate your fears

When your worries become too much, pause and find the root of this worry. Most of the time, it stems from a fear that something is going to happen. Your fears are usually coming from worries that you haven't acknowledged yet. Ask yourself, "Am I predicting the future? Am I doubting that I will be able to handle whatever happens next?" Most of the time, we underestimate our abilities to gain control of ourselves and handle situations. Sometimes you just have to face the fears, challenge your thoughts, and let whatever happens happen. More often than not, you will see the circumstance was not as bad as you thought.

6. Practice meditation

learN

Meditation is one of the most effective relaxation strategies. When we are relaxed, it is easier for our brains to unwind and shut down for a while. Most meditation focuses on our breathing. Through meditation, you can learn how to breathe effectively, where to breathe from, and to be more aware of how you are breathing when out and about. Although meditation may not do something for you right now if you are expecting immediate relief, I can assure you that you will feel more at peace over time. Meditation is not just a quick fix to calming you down, but a long-term, effective solution in training your mind to handle stressful situations better. A peaceful, calm mind is a happy, calm soul. When our souls are peaceful, our lives are also peaceful.

7. Develop positive self-talk

When you have a nagging, worried mind, it usually means that you are not giving yourself credit for the stressful things you have been through before. Develop this thought when you get panicked: *I have gotten through harder and worse situations than this before, so I am fully capable of handling what I am facing*

46

now. Try to replace your doubting thoughts with healthy mantras for quick, in-the-moment relief. If you catch yourself saying, "I don't know if I can do this," then replace it with, "I know I can." When you catch yourself thinking, "I hope he or she doesn't judge me," then replace it with, "I am confident," or, "I am resilient." Even if you do not believe in the positive things you tell yourself, the longer and more frequently you think them, the more your mind will develop these positive ways, and the less likely your worries will be negative.

8. Replace your worries with truths

When you worry about the past or the future, replace these worries with: "*All we have is now; I cannot control yesterday, and I cannot predict tomorrow.*" By replacing your worries or fears with the truth, you will find yourself able to stay calm in the present moment. Most of the time, we worry about things out of our control, attempt to predict the future, or stress too much about what is happening right now. If you are in a meeting and your mind begins to worry about how you are not going to be good or do good, then say to yourself, "Look at me, I am doing fine so far. If I mess up, I can and will be able to fix it." By reinforcing positive thoughts and replacing worries with truth, your worries decrease, and you will automate this strategy over time.

9. "What if's" don't matter; "How can I's" do

When you stress about, "What if the house burns down?" Or, "What if I didn't unplug the lava lamp?" Or, "What if I forgot something?" Instead, think, "How possible is it that my house burns down? How can I solve the lava lamp problem? How can I manage if I forgot something?" Do you see the difference when you change "what if" to "how can I"? Most of the time our "what if" worries are exaggerated, irrational, and sometimes even illogical.

10. Accept the unknown

The unknown is a certain thing that we all face. It is sort of like thinking and stressing over things we cannot control because we don't know what is going to happen. Too many people NEED to know everything and plan it all out. Try developing the strategy to just be. Just understand that unexpected things happen, so hope for the best and don't expect much more than that. plan for worst

In conclusion, our worries stem into fears, which give us anxiety. When we get anxious, we forget to use our logical minds, and then our worries take over and send us into a spiral of out-of-control thinking. By developing and improving these effective strategies to overcome over-worried minds, you will find that you have less anxiety and are able to "control" more things around you, including yourself.

STEP 3: DEALING WITH NEGATIVE THOUGHTS

Negative thoughts are similar to worrying and overthinking, except the biggest difference is when you are just plain negative. Sure, you may worry, but what takes up most of your mind and thoughts are the negative things you tell yourself. The thing negative thinking and worrying have in common is that they both need acknowledgment. As stated in the previous chapter, you cannot just wait for them to disappear, push them away, ignore them, or pretend they aren't that bad. Why? Because they get worse. It's like an annoying sibling: They will poke you repeatedly until you snap or deal with them.

So, how exactly do you deal with negative thoughts? You have to acknowledge that they are there and pay attention to them. Pick them apart and find the root of where they are coming from. The truth about avoidance is no matter what you avoid or how much you try to prevent something, it either goes away and comes back, or it gets more dominant and lasts longer. For example, if you tell yourself, "I'm not going to be like 'so and so,'" or, "I will never be or do 'whatever,'" and then do everything in your power to avoid being or acting like a certain person or even doing a specific task, it may come full circle without you even noticing. You may then end up doing the thing you said you would never do or acting like the person you said you would never imitate. Negative thoughts work this way, so stop avoiding them!

A more effective way to handle negative thoughts is to become observant of them. If your thought is, "I am not good enough, and I never will be," then all you have to do is notice it. Don't judge this as negative or positive. Don't question it or define it. Just watch it. Once you have taken a moment to see and feel this negative thought, explore it. So, look at what's happening in your life and with yourself. Maybe the feeling of not being good enough stems from the fact that you have failed in things you were trying to do or the job you were trying to get. Pinpoint the reason and challenge it with, "I didn't get the job I wanted, so it's fair to think that I am not good enough, but that doesn't mean there are no other opportunities out there in the same field. I can always explore other options if I want to." Once you have observed, paused for a moment, identified the thought, and explored why you would think that, then see how you feel after you have taken these steps. You will probably feel more productive and maybe even feel better.

What I just explained is called **Acceptance and Commitment Therapy** (or **ACT**[1]). If you noticed, the great thing about ACT is that you don't ignore or change your thoughts. Instead, you change how you view and react to them.

Among ACT, there are other small things you can do to decrease negative thinking:

Switch your focus to something positive

If you focus on funny memes, look up funny sayings, or talk to a positive influence, then your attention won't be so focused on your negative thoughts. This does not mean avoiding them, but just switching your focus until you have time to address them later. Concentrate on changing your mind to happy memories or whatever makes you smile.

Practice self-love

Someone close to me used to say, "When you work and get your paycheck, put 10% away or use that 10% on something for yourself." I started doing this, and I slowly started to feel better. We are always so worried about taking care of our bills, rent, food, or taking care of others, that we forget about ourselves. Self-love is about treating yourself the way you would treat your close friends or a family member. When your negative thoughts persist, respond to them as you would if someone close to you told you these things.

Stop changing behaviors or habits to appease your negativity

You may have developed an avoidance behavior as a result of trying to stop your negative thoughts from happening. When your negative thoughts come out of nowhere or are triggered by things, they are called intrusive thoughts. An example of behavioral change involving intrusive thoughts may look like one of these:

If you experience violent thoughts around knives or when you are holding a knife, then you may get rid of knives or just never touch them.

If you experience intrusive thoughts around children, then you may limit your interaction with them, be extra careful about how you look at them, and even avoid changing or bathing them.

If one of these sounds about right, then you need to stop.

The more you feed into the fear of something happening revolving around your intrusive thoughts, the more they will take over and eventually get worse, potentially to the point where you may avoid leaving your house. When you stop, you may find that your thoughts don't control you and they will go away on their own, as this is your way of "proving them wrong," in a sense. Your thoughts are not going to force you to do anything as they are just words and sentences mixed together to disturb your mind. Only you define what you are going to do with your actions.

What Happens in the Mind Involving our Negative Thoughts

In the Journal of Clinical Psychology, there was a study revolving around the effects of worrying and negative thinking surrounding a task. Participants were asked to sort things into two categories. People who worried 50% of the time or more showed an increased difficulty to sort the object into the two categories. This study shows how negative thinking weakens the ability to process information, as well as the ability to think clearly. This means that thinking negatively about problems doesn't solve anything and can actually make things more difficult due to the unclear thought-patterns surrounding negative thinking.

Amygdala

Most times, people cannot control their negative thought-patterns, and this is because, over long periods, our brain shapes itself and changes based on the way we think and perceive things. The amygdala, as talked about in the previous chapter, is where the brain stores negative experiences and is responsible for the "fight, flight, freeze" response.

Here is a good example of how the amygdala comes into play: Someone who is stuck in traffic can be stressed due to the level of threat to their safety, if they are going to be late for work or to pick someone up, or if there was a car accident ahead. The "threat" doesn't seem that threatening to them, rather an annoyance where they can easily talk themselves out of the fear that anything bad is going to happen.

On the other hand, for someone in this exact same situation who has been previously exposed to stress surrounding a traffic jam, car accident, or any negative experiences involving this circumstance, it will trigger the amygdala to send signals to the body as if this person were in the fight-or-flight mode. Because of negative experiences piling up in the amygdala, this part of the brain cannot tell the difference between false-alarm threats and real threats, so it is kicked into overdrive. This happens because of the overuse of negative thinking over extended periods of time.

Thalamus

The thalamus is responsible for the sensory and motor signals in the brain. It sends these signals to the rest of the body but cannot decipher the difference between real danger and false alarms. The amygdala and the thalamus work together to create or diminish stress responses to the rest of the body based on the way you think or control your thinking. False alarms are your amygdala telling your thalamus that there is danger. Your thalamus then sends adrenaline signals to the rest of your body to get you ready to fight or flee from the danger your brain is signaling. It can happen out of nowhere and only happens based on the negative thought-patterns you have accumulated over some time.

Changes in Cortisol

Cortisol is your brain's stress component. It controls mood, motivation, and fear. Higher increases of cortisol stem from mental disorders, such as anxiety, depression, ADHD, PTSD, and other mood disorders. People who have mental disorders, compared to people who do not, show higher levels of cortisol hormones, which is why it is much more difficult for these people to calm down. There are other abnormalities in their brains, such as white and grey matter. Grey matter is **where** information is processed, and white matter is **when** the neurons in your brain **connect** this information to where it needs to go in the brain. Chronic stress, increased cortisol levels, and low dopamine and serotonin levels all contribute to the production of more white matter connections.

When white and grey matter are balanced, the parts of the brain responsible for mood and memories, like the hippocampus, become undisturbed, which results in less "triggers" from the thalamus sending false-alarm signals to the body. You can balance this white and grey matter when you practice positive thinking and change negative habits. You would train your brain in this way by rewarding yourself for good behavior and creating self-disciplinary techniques. For example, if you fear walking alone to the store, then discipline yourself by walking halfway to the store alone and talking on the phone the rest of the way, the whole time telling yourself you can do it and it's not scary. Reward yourself when you complete small milestones towards your goal, eventually building up to a big reward when you finally walk all the way to and from the store alone.

Removing Toxicity

Negative thinking mostly has to do with the way you live your life. If you are around positive influences, then you are more likely to develop positive thinking. However, if you surround yourself with negative environments and toxic people, then you are more likely to develop negative thoughts and feelings. Have you ever just sat there, and felt tense for no reason - or seemingly no reason? Maybe you have just accepted that you are a tense person and it's impossible for you to relax. This is because you have gotten used to the toxicity in your life. Toxicity comes from everywhere and almost everything, if you are not careful. You can be in a toxic relationship, be renting from a toxic landlord, working for a toxic employer, or be best friends with a toxic person. Whatever it is, you must figure out if you are in a toxic situation and start making arrangements for removing yourself from it.

Here are seven actions you can take to remove toxicity in your life:

1. Analyze your situation

Analyze your circumstances to find the root of the toxicity. For example, figure out when the last time you felt at peace, even if it was for a single moment. Was it at your mom's house? What were you thinking in this moment? Where is your happy place? What does inner harmony feel like to you? Next, figure out in your situation, of where you are in your life right now, what is missing to have this inner peace? If negativity stems from the person you are living with, then figure out what it is about this person that is so negative and how you can break free of it. If the negativity is because you are tense or stressed about your landlord, then find out how you can break free of their attachment to you or your attachment to them. Whatever the toxicity is, you must take action right away. Procrastinating is only going to bring on more fear involving the toxicity.

2. Replace negative things with positive things

Once you have identified the toxic situations in your life, it is time to replace these negative circumstances with positive ones. For example, if you feel stressed at home and it is hard to feel relief, then make it a habit to go for a run or do something rewarding for yourself every day. That may be getting yourself your favorite coffee or going to your favorite dog park or beach. If your social circle is bringing you toxicity, then it is time to go online and meet more people. If meeting people is hard for you, then remind yourself that meeting positive influences will help you find a sense of being in finding who you are and want to be. Try to look at the glass as half-full, rather than half-empty. Maybe it's your workplace that you feel most stressed. If so, start looking for a different job or do hobbies after work that fulfill your inner desire.

3. Find your purpose or a purpose

Find positivity in your life, even if it is small. If your friends aren't supportive of your dreams or you seem to be surrounded by selfish people who "suck the life" out of you, then the positive in this is that you are not selfish. If you think you are being taken for granted, then it only means you have more empathy than you give yourself credit for, and you can sympathize with yourself and others to see the positive. When you wake up, be blessed that you woke another day and you aren't in the hospital with a disease. When you eat a good meal, be thankful for the fact that you have eaten something today. Many times we forget that so many other people are suffering far more than we are. We forget the benefits we have and take even the smallest things for granted. Be thankful that you wanted to buy and were able to afford this book - it means you want to learn and make great changes. Change your perspective and live a life full of gratitude, as some people do not get this benefit.

4. Find your passion and your desire

The reason most people take on negative thinking and the excessive worries, stemming from overthinking, is because most people aren't actually living a life they deserve or love. If you are working in an environment or even a job that you hate, but the reason you do it is because it pays the bills, then you are not living a passionate life. Think about the things you do that other people seem to struggle with. Are you good at writing? Are you good at communicating? Are you a natural at baking or cooking? Whatever you're great at and that takes no effort is the direction you need to start. Finding your passion and striving to be better will fulfill self-compassion and you will begin to feel happier, resulting in the removal of toxicity. When you do what you love, nothing else will matter because it is something you do that you will always look forward to.

5. Reward yourself often

As discussed in the previous chapter, dopamine is the brain chemical that releases endorphins which makes you feel good. It is important to reward yourself, even for the small things, as it releases dopamine. When you wake up and feel grateful, acknowledge this feeling and reward yourself with a simple, "Good job, I woke up feeling grateful for … I am going to keep practicing this." These self-talks can encourage higher dopamine levels which creates a healthy habit to become more positive. Also, in rewarding yourself, take pleasure in taking a break. When life becomes too stressful or you feel yourself losing control, take a mindful moment to bring yourself to a happy feeling or memory and embrace this moment as if nothing else exists or matters. Everything else can wait because the most important thing in this world is making yourself happy. When you are happy, the world can smile along with you. Go on a nature walk often as this allows your brain to take in the sights and smells of natural, healing sensations.

6. Be okay with mistakes

Remind yourself that there is not going to be an immediate change. Change happens for many people, and the more you practice, the better you will become. Sometimes change isn't as noticeable as we would like. For example, I remember being negative and I didn't think I would get any better. I started changing my life and my surroundings. I developed better eating habits, started going on brisk walks every day, and tried to be aware of my thought-patterns throughout the day. Whenever a negative thought popped into my head, I noticed it and challenged it with truth and reflection. The situation I was in wasn't helping me and I didn't feel like I was getting any better, so I moved and rede-veloped a sense of home in my own place. I didn't notice anything until I went back and visited the roommates I used to live with; they were in the same pattern as always and I had realized that I was stronger and didn't think at all the way I used to when I lived with them.

As you can see, change may not come easy and it may go

unnoticed, but it does happen. Everyone has bad days, so on these days, just be patient with yourself and accept that it is okay to have one, two, or maybe even three bad days in a row. Accept that mistakes happen, and failure is the only way to strive forward. We don't learn from our healthy habits, rather we learn from making these mistakes as it teaches us something new every time and reminds us why we should develop healthy habits.

7. Seek professional help

When nothing seems to be going right, you keep making mistakes and you feel like you have fallen further down than when you had started, sometimes, professional help can work best. Therapists, doctors, naturopaths, and clinical counselors can point you in the right direction and give you helpful coping techniques to get you started for positivity. Often, anxiety or other mood disorders take over our minds, and it becomes more difficult to get up and want to try every day. So maybe the root problem is not your thoughts but something deeper. Only a professional will be able to get you unstuck and headed towards the path you want.

Toxicity is crucial to remove from our lives because it can weigh us down and trigger more negative thinking. When we don't remove or make an effort to remove toxicity, we don't give ourselves a fair chance to succeed.

STEP 4: HOW TO CONTROL OVERTHINKING AND ELIMINATE NEGATIVE THOUGHTS IN JUST A FEW MINUTES

One thing that overthinking, worrying, and negative thinking have in common is that they are all mental chatter or mental noise. They are thoughts that disturb our inner and outer peace. Regardless of the scientific reasons behind them, it is mental noise that becomes embedded in your mind over time. Most times, it is uncontrollable - or we think it is uncontrollable - and it often comes out of nowhere when we are in a place mentally and/or physically that we cannot seem to get out of. However, thoughts and mental chatter can be a good thing when used for productive things, like planning, studying, and analyzing. It's when the thoughts don't have an off-switch that makes it hard to fall or stay asleep and intensifies stress, worry, anger, or other uncomfortable feelings.

We have already discussed in the previous chapters what each of these mental chatter noises involve, but here is a recap of what they are and how to identify them:

• Negative thoughts or consistent worries that become repetitive;

• Reliving or repetitive images or "movies" that revolve around past experiences or fears;

• Fretting about the past or fearing the unknown uncertainties, distracting us from the present moment;

• Unable to focus on conversations in the present because our minds are constantly thinking about too many things, like tasks we need to do;

• Constant worrying about what people think of us, so we strive for perfection. Our perfections never seem good enough because our mental chatter never allows us to achieve these goals;

• Involuntary thinking and daydreaming. We overanalyze every situation and stress about the things we are unsure about because we fear the future and overthink about what we can't change.

These types of thought-patterns are unhealthy, and this is why affected people seem tired and exhausted 90% of the time. In this chapter, I will explain how you can discipline your mind into switching this type of mental chatter off. I will teach you how to reboot your mind so that you can rest easier at night and get some silence when you want to relax. One of the main ways to shut off mental noise is to endure, learn, and practice concentration exercises. Just like all the other techniques explained throughout this book, it is not going to happen overnight, but the more you practice, the quieter your mind will get. Eventually it will become second nature to switch your thinking on and off as if it were a switch.

Calming Your Mind

Calming your mind is a special skill that takes determination, consistency, and patience. The reason why it is beneficial to quiet your mind is because so many advantages come from having peace within yourself. When you find peace on the inside, it will become easier to find peace outside of you in every situation and environment you surround yourself with. The goal behind inner peace and a quiet mind isn't to stop thinking, but to surpass the barriers your mind keeps you trapped in. Here are five secrets to finding inner peace and quieting the mind:

1. Listen to and watch the mental noise your thoughts bring you

Watch your thoughts without labeling them. If an intrusive, disturbing thought pops up like, "I wish I were good enough," or, "I want to hurt myself," then do not judge it or label it as good, bad, scary, threatening, or anything negative. Notice it and allow it to be there. Don't push it away or avoid it. Don't think about where it came from, but embrace that it is there. When you do this, it weakens the power your thoughts have over you, and you gain control of yourself and your worries.

2. Consciously and purposely challenge your thoughts

This technique revolves around cognitive behavioral therapy. Many psychologists swear by this method because it means that you can control or alter your thoughts to another direction and create new patterns or habits of the way you interact with your thoughts. You take control back by challenging them. Start by asking yourself about your thoughts. So, if your thought is that you aren't good enough, then ask yourself where this comes from. Are you jumping to conclusions? Which one of the cognitive distortions does this thought fall under? Next, find the positive. What has happened in your life that makes you feel as if you are not good enough? Finding the root of the thought of where it's coming from can really give you insight for taking your control back because you can then replace it with the truth.

3. Intentionally focus on your breathing

Oftentimes, we get anxious, worried, or set off our "false alarm" triggers because we aren't breathing properly. Close your eyes and focus on where your breath is coming from: your stomach, your chest, or your nose. Next, just practice noticing your breath without changing it. Once you have figured out where your breath is coming from and how you are breathing, you can then focus on taking in deep, long breaths. Count your inhale to five seconds, hold for three seconds, and exhale for five-to-seven seconds. Repeat until you feel calmer, and then go back to normal breathing before you open your eyes again.

4. Play calming music that relaxes and motivates you

Music is one of the best healers out there. When we can relate to the singer, they become our favorite artist, and then we can feel more relaxed knowing that they are singing about something that means something to you. If instrumental is more your thing, then just pay attention to the rhythm and the noise the instruments make. Close your eyes and try to concentrate on any background noises you may not have noticed before. Try to name the instruments and memorize the tune.

5. Participate in regular exercise

When we exercise on a daily basis, it releases those "feel good" chemicals we previously talked about. When dopamine is released, it becomes easier for our brain to produce more serotonin, allowing us to feel happy. When we are happy, we don't feel so stressed, and our thoughts don't become so overwhelming or overpowering. The idea is to work our bodies physically, so our minds don't have the energy to overthink or create mental chatter.

When we overthink, worry excessively, or think negatively all the time, mental chatter becomes worse, and it can seem impossible to fix. In the next section, I will discuss techniques on how to reboot your brain.

Brain Reboot

The best way to overcome negative thinking, worrying, and overthinking is to reset the brain. First, you need to be able to accept change and overcome your fears that the thoughts bring into your mind. Secondly, you need to be willing to learn how to change your state of mind and the way you think. The biggest question is: **How** do we do this? Most of the "rebooting" process is what we have already talked about. However, the objective of the other techniques was to stop the overthinking patterns. Now, the primary reason most people have an overactive mind is because there is a lot more information to process in today's society compared to three decades ago. Today, we have social networking, technology, and loads of new information that we interpret and interact with daily.

When you read these next techniques on how to reboot your brain, think about the objective, as you are discovering how you can reset the mind, not how to stop or lessen your thoughts.

1. Stop multitasking

Although multitasking can be a good thing, this is one reason why our brain operates on overdrive. When we try to focus, think about, or do too many things at once, it means that our brains are switching focus from one thing to the next, then to the next. This way of thinking actually weakens the ability to get multiple things done at once. For example, do you find when you clean your house that you start with the dishes, then you move on to vacuuming before the dishes are done, then you continue to wipe the counters and find yourself sweeping or mopping the floors twice? You may find that after all that work, you are more exhausted. When you look around, you still have laundry or more dishes to do, and it looks as if you barely did anything. This is the effect of multitasking.

Multitasking creates a shorter attention span and a distracted mind, also known as the "monkey brain" or the "squirrel effect." To stop multitasking, try focusing on one thing at a time and make sure you do not move on to the next thing until that one task is completed.

2. Concentrate on a single thing at a time

The author of the book called *The Organized Mind: Thinking Straight in the Age of Information Overload,* Daniel Levitin, promotes Deliberate Immersion. Deliberate Immersion means that we split our tasks or duties into time-slots of no more than 30-50 minutes at a time without other distractions. Daniel Levitin says there are two modes of attention that our brains are composed of: The task-positive and the task-negative networks. The task-positive network is the ability to complete tasks without distractions from the outside world or the environment around you, like television, conversations with people you love in the home, or your phone going off distracting you with social media and what's going on outside the home. The negative-task network is when your mind is actively daydreaming or wandering, not focusing on the task at hand. It means that you are busy thinking about other things while you are trying to complete a chore. The negative-task network is where creativity and inspiration stem from. Then, we have an "attention filter," which is responsible for switching between the two modes. It helps us stay organized and lets us keep the focus on the current mode we are in, allowing us to complete the given chore we are doing.

3. "Attention Filter"

In short, Daniel Levitin says that if you want to be more creatively productive, then you should set aside a time for your social tasks when you are trying to complete a focused or attentive task. This means that there is always a time and place for things like status updates, Twitter, text messages, where you left your wallet, or how to reconcile an argument with a spouse or friend. When you set aside social aspects to a designated time-period of the day, you will be less distracted and get more things done, which is a great way to reboot the brain when you focus on just ONE thing. The time for task-negative networking (daydreaming, mind wandering, or deep thinking) is when you go on nature walks, listen to music while checking social statuses, or bathing with aromatherapy while possibly reading a book. When we implement mind wandering with these activities, it actually resets our brains and provides different and healthier perspectives on what we are doing or going to do.

The Four Steps to Mindfulness

Mindfulness is a great method for resetting the brain in the moment. When you find yourself having "squirrel" moments or have a difficult time turning off the "monkey mind," return to mindfulness. Mindfulness helps with deeper relaxation techniques - much like meditation, sleep, and concentration. Here are the four steps to practicing mindfulness effectively:

Relabel

Relabeling consists of stepping back and addressing the thought, feeling, or behavior. Ask yourself, which cognitive distortion does this thought fall under? Which feeling can you attach this thought to? What does this thought and feeling make you want to do? Why? When you identify these messages, you will be able to better understand where they come from and when they are "false alarms."

Reattribute

Once you have identified the message your thought, feeling, or behavior brings to the surface, you must reassign the thought to a different perspective. Figure out how important the thought is. If it is important or repetitive, then add a new definition behind it and see it in a different light.

Refocus

Once you have addressed the thought, picked it apart, added meaning, and changed your perception, switch your focus. The point of this is to not get stuck thinking about this for too long, as that is why your brain becomes overactive and scattered. It is when you intentionally switch your focus to something else that rewires and resets your brain.

Revalue

Revaluing happens when you have mastered the other three steps. It happens almost instantly after some time. Revaluing means you can see thoughts, urges, and impulses for what they are. When you see these things for what they are, you will have reset your brain to configure and place your thoughts in the correct "brain slots." Your brain will automatically be able to decipher whether a thought or message is beneficial or destructive.

To recap, the easiest way to reboot the brain is to stop multi-tasking, notice when you are processing or taking on too many tasks or too much information, switch thinking about things to healthy distractions, be mindful of your thoughts, and practice focusing your attention to one thing at a time.

Analysis Paralysis

"Analysis paralysis or paralysis by analysis is an anti-pattern, the state of over-analyzing (or overthinking) a situation so that a decision or action is never taken, in effect paralyzing the outcome."[1]

I like to think of this in relation to the "flight, fight, freeze" response - analysis paralysis being the freeze reaction. This is when a person gets so caught up in their own thoughts about what to do with a solution to a problem that they can't figure out which solution to choose, so instead they do nothing. Analysis paralysis stems from decision-making skills. American psychologist, Herbert Simon, says that we make decisions in one of two ways:

Satisfice

This means that people pick one option that best suits their needs or attention.

Maximize

This means that people cannot be satisfied with one decision but make up multiple solutions and always think there are better alternatives than their original decision.

Maximizers are the ones who suffer with analysis paralysis the most. People overthink because they fear their potential mistakes and want to avoid the possibility of failure. Analysis paralysis is a fancy word for overthinking combined with the inability to make decisions.

Overcoming Analysis Paralysis

Since analysis paralysis stems from the inability to make effective and quick decisions, the way to overcome it is to simply work on your decision-making skills. Here are ways to get unstuck when you have developed overthinking to the point of analysis paralysis:

1. Prioritize your decisions

Break your decisions into categories, meaning you should figure out which decisions are big, and which are small; which are important, and which decisions don't need much attention. When figuring out which decision to put into which category, ask yourself these questions:

• How important is this decision?

• How immediate is the decision I need to make?

• Is this decision going to make a big or small impact on what happens next?

• What are the best-case and worst-case scenarios based on the solutions I have come up with?

When we categorize our decisions, it makes it easier to stick to our final decision without changing our minds later.

2. Find the "end goal" as part of your solution

When you are stuck wondering **why** you need to make a decision, you can get stuck in the analysis-paralysis trap. Our decisions can revolve around many other thoughts, like "What if I make the wrong choice?" or, "There are so many things I can do, but which is the right decision to make?" If not knowing **why** you need to make a decision is the case for you, then defining the goal or objective may be a better way to look at the decision you need to make. For example, imagine you are stuck between choosing between two jobs, you already have a career you are succeeding in, but you want something new and are unsure why you need to make a decision or even if you should. Ask yourself what the objective is - where do you envision you should or will be five-to-ten years from now? When you look at the "end goal," it may become easier to figure out what you need to do.

3. Break decisions into smaller portions

This technique is like the opposite of the last technique. You are still looking at the "end goal," but instead of making a decision based on the end goal, you are breaking your end goal into a smaller goal. You can then break your decisions into smaller decisions to complete the "mini goal(s)." While this is still decision-making, make sure that when you come to a final decision, you stick with it. If you are still having a

hard time deciding, then write your decisions
paper and come up with no more than three-tc
sions. Eventually, the more you do this, the smaller the list
will become every time and you will only make one decision,
which is a goal inside itself - to overcome analysis paralysis.

4. Get a second opinion

If you are still stuck after you have made your list and you
are still overthinking the many things you can do, then pick
two top solutions and bring them up to a trustee. In doing
this, let go of all judgements within yourself. Let go of
control and perfectionism. Rely solely on this other person's
opinion, and if they give you advice on a decision you are
still unsure about or may not have chosen in the end, then
remind yourself that you came to them because you were
struggling, and you trust them. Ask yourself how many
times this person may have been right when you went
against them. Also, tell yourself that you need to let go of
the fear that something bad will happen. A quote that has
made a big impact on me, as well as the people in my life, is
this: *"Insanity: doing the same thing over and over again and expecting
different results"*.[2] In other words, if you continue to do the
same thing but you're expecting something different, then
the change will never happen.

Fear

A big part of overthinking, worrying, and negative thinking
all revolves around one thing: Fear. Fear of losing control,
fear of making a mistake or failing, fear of making a deci-

sion, or just a general fear. Fear is learned and can be solved with self-discipline and exposure therapy. Fear is paralyzing and can actually stop someone from doing what they want, making people miss out on successful opportunities. Fear is the number one response to excessive worries and over-thinking brains. In order to feel completely in control of our thoughts and actions, it is best to overcome our fears.

Here are some techniques for overcoming fear:

1. Acknowledge that the fear (no matter how big or small) is real

When people have fear or are anxious about a specific thing or a variety of things, the fear is real for them. Fear is often a good thing to have; it means that our human instincts are working properly. For example, a woman who is walking home after work in the dark by herself should have worries or fears about walking alone in the dark. A child's first day of school can be worrisome and fearful, as well as for a child or student who enters a new school in the middle of the year. A man who has to go into surgery on their brain or another functioning organ, or someone who needs to go to the dentist, both fear the potential for a bad outcome. These are all fears that **should** be there. However, a fear of clowns, small spaces, flying, or heights are all irrational fears or fears that have been learned. Whatever someone fears is real to them and should be looked at with appreciation and never forced to overcome. Fears cannot be overcome unless the person is willing to tackle them.

2. Accept your fear

Accept that you have this fear. This could be as big as starting a new job, meeting new people, moving to a new town or city, or becoming a parent. Or it could be as small as a spider that scurries across your feet, weird creaking noises in your new house, someone scaring you, or driving. Whatever it is that makes you fearful, accept that this is the fear you have; don't ignore it, avoid it, or deny it. It's there, and you fear it.

3. Break it down

Gain some perspective on your fear. Ask yourself:

• What risk are you at?

• Can having this fear really hurt you?

• If your fear came true, then what would happen?

• What are the best-case and the worst-case scenarios if this fear were to be right in front of you, right now?

Sometimes fears are irrational and cause many people to overthink. Other times overthinking causes new fears to evolve. So once you have asked yourself those questions, ask some more:

• If the scenario happened (worst case), what could you do about it?

• Do you underestimate your ability to handle the situation?

• If the scenario happened (best case), what could you do about it?

• Do you overestimate your ability to handle the situation?

Oftentimes, people share the same fears. Find someone you share your fears with and strive to overcome them together. When you share the same fears as someone else, you feel a sense of belonging, as you are not alone in these fears.

4. Give into the fear - assuming the worst

The best way to overcome your fears is to face them or to mindfully pay attention to them. For a while, I had anxiety about going out in public. So when I was faced with a public situation, like grocery shopping, I would become overwhelmed and the physical symptoms of fear would kick in - much like a panic attack. When I intentionally went out in public, I first watched my thoughts, and if they were negative, then I would challenge them and replace them with better ones. If my fear became overwhelming, I would go home, but I would try again when I had calmed down - usually the next day. I didn't let fear take control because I kept fighting back. This is also called exposure therapy.

Exposure Therapy

Exposure therapy does not work for everyone, however, when you dedicate yourself to continuing to try even when fear takes over, you will succeed in overcoming the very thing you are afraid of. Exposure therapy is what a psychologist will introduce to someone who suffers from a panic disorder or some other mood disorder.

It is a type of therapy that helps people with mood disorders to confront their irrational fears. However, you do not need to have a disability if you want to use exposure therapy, as it works for anyone who is willing to learn. There are different types of exposure therapies, including:

In vivo exposure

This is facing a feared object, situation, or activity head-on in real-life scenarios. For example, someone who fears public transit may be advised to go on a bus or monorail (first with someone, then without someone). Someone who fears social interaction may be advised to present a speech in front of a small group of people, building up to an assembly of people.

Imaginal exposure

This is when you sit with a trusted friend or a psychologist and let them guide you visually with your feared object, situation, or activity. For example, someone with PTSD would go through a guided visualization of the things that had happened to them revolving around their fear from their past. Over time, their fear doesn't affect them as badly.

Virtual reality exposure

When other exposures are not practical or helpful, this is when virtual reality is used. For example, someone who fears flying may take a virtual or guided visualization of flying. This virtual world brings the person into the world of flying, without actually flying, experiencing the sights, sounds, smells, and texture of their surroundings.

Interoceptive exposure

This is the use of intentionally bringing about the physical sensations of the feared sensation. For example, someone with a panic disorder may get more heightened fear when they feel dizzy from a panic attack. They may be instructed to spin in circles to exaggerate the effects, and then try to stand, keep their balance, or sit down. This is so they understand that the physical effects are not as scary when it's happening because they can implement the same feelings themselves.

Exposure therapy helps people overcome their fears because it develops and rewires the brain to make different connections. When people intentionally create or face their fear, the fear only becomes a distant memory and therefore has no control over the person.

STEP 5: APPLYING POSITIVITY

The thing about positive thinking is that it is contagious, just like negative thinking. Meaning, when you are around a positive person, you can take on this "vibe" or energy and become positive yourself. Positivity affects more than just you; it affects the people and environment around you. For example, if you were to go to a job interview and you showed up with a confident, positive attitude, then the employer would be more inclined to hire you. If you showed up tired, hungry, or exhausted, then this would show in your attitude and you wouldn't be able to put your best foot forward. The employer would most likely turn a blind eye to you and hire the next positive person that came for an interview. It's simple - positive attracts positive, and negative attracts negative.

As discussed in the previous chapters, it has been proven that our brains actually change shape and form depending on how we think and live our lives. With that being said, what's more interesting is that when we repeat habits, thoughts, and behaviors, we are actually training our brain. We can train our brain to act and behave in any way we want because when we repeat things, our brains connect synapses that weren't previously there and then associate these thoughts with behaviors, turning them into habits. So it makes sense to say that when we think negatively, we are repeating bad thoughts to ourselves. While our brain associates the negative thoughts with the behaviors that we act on, we then continue to repeat bad habits. We can do this with positive thinking as well. Ever heard the saying: "Life is what you make it?" This is true due to the fact that when we implement negative thoughts, we act, see, feel, and apply negative habits. However, when we repeat positive things to ourselves (even when we don't believe them), we start to see, hear, think, and apply positive behaviors.

The reason negativity is mostly seen in this generation or society is because negativity is addictive. It's hard to escape, and once we think negatively, we cannot stop as it acts like a drug. We do these things because we don't like to take blame; instead, we want to blame our negative thoughts for why we are depressed. We blame our worrying for why we are anxious. We blame our overthinking for our actions. It's a hard truth to accept, but the only person to blame for your negative thinking is YOU. The thing is, change isn't easy. What's easy is what we continue to do, what is familiar to us. So it's no wonder we don't just wake up one day and say, "Hey, I am going to be positive today." But that is the answer, it's your choice to wake up and be positive, and it really is that easy. However, what is not easy is continuing to do something new and different. This is why changing and rewiring your brain to be positive takes commitment and dedication if you truly want to escape the nightmare of negativity you have been living in.

How to Think Positive

When you develop and improve positive thinking, it goes beyond just what you think about that makes you smile. It becomes your environment. It becomes who you are as an individual. Positivity - just like negativity - consumes us. It can be very difficult to think positively when having a rough day or when everyone or everything around you seems depressing or worrisome. But the truth is, when you think positively, your aura and mind stop looking for the bad in every situation and you actually become grateful for these hard days and extreme failures because they shape your destiny. In every horrible scenario, there is good that you can take from it. At first, seeing the positive in situations can be very difficult, but over time, it will become so easy that you won't even need to think, the positive will just be there.

So, how do we do it? Here are four ways you can develop positivity in your life:

1. Focus on three (or more) positive things daily

Before going to sleep at night, rehash your day in your mind. Think about everything that happened and take three positive perceptions away from the day. It could be anything. Was the sun shining? Did you reconnect with an old friend? Maybe your boss or co-worker wasn't that grumpy today which made it a less stressful day. The more you start seeing the small positive effects, the more your perception of positivity will develop, and the quicker happiness and success will come.

2. Do something nice for someone

It may not seem like it, but acts of kindness can not only lift your spirits but lift someone else's spirits as well. When we do nice for others, we are actually feeding our soul with positivity because those chemical endorphins shoot off in our brains as a reward response. These acts could be anything, such as smiling at a stranger, waving to a coworker, or pausing to do something thoughtful for someone you know. When you make someone else smile, your heart smiles, which makes you feel better about your-self and develop confidence.

3. Be in the present

If I haven't said this enough, then let me say it again: Be mindful! When we stay in the present moment, it creates balance and structure in our own awareness of what is going on around us. When we become aware of our surroundings while staying in the present moment, we will be able to better pick up on the positive things that happen, and nega-tivity will seem like a distant friend.

4. Practice self-love and gratitude

The thing about positivity is that when you love yourself, it becomes easier to help others and give back to the universe. Just think about it - if you don't love yourself, then your relationships fall apart faster, your job never seems to feel satisfying, and you constantly second-guess your ability to handle stressful situations. However, when you do love yourself, you can be thankful for what you have because you have it. You won't be asking for more or for things that you don't have, and envy or jealousy won't seem like important things to worry about anymore. Being grateful for the human you are requires self-acceptance and a deeper understanding of what you want in life. So, any chance you get, be grateful for what you have rather than envy what you don't have. *The grass is rarely greener on the other side.*

Changing Your Mood

Most of the time, we get stuck in negative thought-patterns because our moods are dark. It's a cycle - negative or worrisome thoughts bring on bad moods, which bring on perceptions of more negative outcomes, which then makes it hard to make important decisions because our minds are crowded, which then leads to overthinking (or negative thoughts), and so on. Some days we don't want to get out of bed, and other days we are motivated, producing "feel good" chemicals that result in getting more done. On the days you feel down, stressed out, anxious, or depressed, think about the productive days and try to draw from that energy. Also, sometimes it is okay to give into your dark mood, just try not to sulk or make it a daily habit.

Here are ways you can change your dark mood to a lighter one when you feel stuck in the mud:

1. Get exercise

We talked about this already as well. When you work out, those "feel good" chemicals release in your brain and can change your mood instantly. Also, it is a good distraction from your bad mood because instead of focusing on what got you so upset, you can focus on other things, like the scenery or your breathing. Make sure to drink water while you work out as being dehydrated can actually make you feel worse.

2. Listen to or watch motivational material

When you don't feel like moving or getting out of bed and it's just one of those days, then watch an inspiring movie or listen to an uplifting podcast. Even though we tend to listen to music that matches what we feel in our down moments, ignore this urge and do the opposite - crank some happy, upbeat tunes. Who knows, it may even want to make you dance or sing. It will lift your spirit 60% faster by listening to or watching motivational material over listening to or watching negative, depressing material. Interestingly, when we listen to what suits our mood at the moment, we are actually training our brains that these attitudes are okay, and then we find ourselves falling deeper into the negative cycle.

3. Change your body language

This means that you should act and behave the way you want to feel. So, if you want to feel confident, then prance around the house in the sexiest or wackiest thing you have and pose in front of a mirror with your chest puffed out and your back straight. If you want to feel relaxed, then throw on your comfy clothes and lounge around, but be mindful of what you tell yourself. Force yourself to smile for 60 seconds, and I guarantee your mood will lift, even if only slightly. Don't let negativity consume you; break free by being you. Be funny, laugh, tickle yourself, talk to someone about your aspirations and dreams, or do whatever you need to get out of the funk you are in and into the mood you want to have.

4. Be grateful or have appreciation for EVERYTHING

Here is a weird, funny fact: We find it normal when someone goes around and complains about everything. We listen to our friends vent, our parents bicker, our bosses complain, and even strangers arguing with themselves some-times. It is "normal" to listen to someone complain and bicker about things, but wouldn't it be weird if we heard someone going off about how grateful and appreciative they are about everything? How often do you hear someone say, "It's raining outside, and I am so grateful for the rain," or, "Food is often taken for granted, so I just wanted to take a moment to feel blessed for this food." Have you ever heard someone say, "I appreciate that my kids scream and give me attitude, because it means they are growing human beings?" No, you probably haven't. Imagine if you said out loud everything you were grateful for today, everything you appreciated today and even yesterday. Imagine how you would feel and how you would make others feel. You may even have a good laugh, but isn't that the point? Practice this.

5. Force positivity, even when you don't feel like it

The truth about your thoughts is that they do not control you. This is the same with moods; they don't control you. So when you have a hard time practicing or enforcing the previous techniques, just do it anyway. Force yourself to smile, force yourself to get out of bed and dance, force yourself to feel grateful. Once you get up and force positivity into your day, you are taking control of your surroundings and your behavior. This teaches your brain that, even in down times and dark moods, you are in control of how you react to them, creating positivity and healthy habits.

Enforcing Positive Habits

Sometimes, thinking positively and changing your mood isn't enough to develop a positive attitude regularly. You have to create habits so that your brain stops synapsing the negative enforcements you have created and starts synapsing the positive ones. While the previous exercises will work in the short-term, you will need to not only practice these every day, but create healthy daily-habits as well. If you stay consistent in creating positive habits, then you will become less anxious, less of a "worry wart," and more easy-going. The minute you know you have succeeded in being positive is when you stop feeling tense during the day and you see the light in all situations. You will feel clear-minded and you will have acceptance of what you can't control, meaning you have acknowledged that negativity no longer consumes you as you have taken the control back.

Let's look at ways you can create positive habits to feel these beneficial results:

1. Find the root of the negativity

Finding the root of your negativity is just the start of what needs to be done before you can continue with your day. Think (but don't think too much) about why you may be in a bad mood or where your negative thoughts are coming from. If they stem from something someone said, then it may be a little easier to get yourself in a better mood, rather than if your negative thoughts stem from continuous behavior surrounding this specific thought. Once you have figured out the root of the negativity, it will be easier to address what to do next.

2. Start the day with positivity

Wake up and be thankful for your life. Be thankful for your kids, your spouse, or the fact that you are not homeless. Be grateful for your friends and family, but most of all, be grateful that you are here, that you got yourself to where you are in life now. Every day that you wake up, do one positive thing that brightens your mood. Do one thing you didn't do yesterday and make this a habit. If you want change, then you have to do something different, so get out of your comfort zone and start the day with positivity. This could be listening to your favorite tunes, making your favorite breakfast, or going for a mindful walk or jog. Remember to always start and finish your day with affirmations for yourself like, "This is going to be a great day," or, "Today was great, and tomorrow will be even better."

3. Find humor in tough situations

If you are having a bad day or you are faced with a negative influence or position, then create an inside joke (to yourself, preferably). You may find that you are funnier than you think, and it is a great way to make light out of a difficult scenario. For example, instead of calling your spouse names in a fight, imagine what would happen if you called them a fruitcake or a wheelbarrow. Picture their face like a tomato or a car wheel. Imagine your thoughts spinning in a tornado of funny memories rather than a spiral of bad images. Maybe you just got fired, so instead of thinking about the financial stresses or all the wrong things that are bound to happen, think of how great it will feel to have just a few days (or weeks) off to yourself. Think about how your next job will be better and shed some light on how ambitious you actually are.

4. Perceive every failure as a lesson to grow

Rather than being fearful of your mistakes, try making mistakes on purpose, just to see what happens. You may find that your mistakes will not only show you what not to do or what to avoid, but they also give you insight on that things are not as bad as you had originally imagined. Most importantly, when you accidentally fail, learn from it. If you messed up at work and got paperwork mixed up or names wrong, then just say sorry and make a mental note to double-check next time. Maybe you forgot a friend's birthday, and it's your best friend who you never forget. Although you feel bad, they might not feel as bad as you may be feeling, so don't beat yourself up about it. Instead, mark it on the calendar for next year and picture yourself doing something really great for them (not just on their birthday, but any day of the year as well).

5. Replace your negative thoughts

For some people, negative thinking is just the way of life for them, so it can be challenging to catch them in a low moment. However, for the times you do catch yourself thinking, "I'm horrible at this," or, "I never do anything right," *then* intentionally make a mental note of these thoughts and simply replace them. Instead think, "I may be bad at this, but with practice I will get better, so I must not give up because I can do this," or, "Just because I feel like I never do anything right, doesn't mean it is true; I am great at many things." When you replace thoughts like this on purpose, you're acknowledging your negative thoughts and creating a habit to think more positively. It is okay if at first you don't believe yourself, but notice the change in your mood after a couple of times doing this.

6. Don't engage in drama

Drama has always excited people, but drama can be pretty harmful when we get caught up in the gossip and eventful turns of our lives or someone else's. When we stop paying attention to these types of events, we can start focusing more on our own lives and do more productive things. Find drama in movies or television, but try to avoid the drama in someone else's life and even your own.

7. Create solutions, not more problems

Problems are what got you into this mess. We are trying to avoid problems by solving them. Solve problems by asking more questions and being engaged with the situation. Be fully in the present rather than in your head. This way, you can handle whatever question or accusation that comes at you. Stay calm and be logical or creative. Listen to your intuition, not your overactive mind. When you are having a difficult time coming up with a logical decision on how to handle something, give yourself (or the person or circumstance) a couple days to process. Journal the problems and "mind map" solutions. Try to come up with no more than three good decisions, and then go to the part in this book that explains how to make decisions (in the next chapter). This is how you will effectively solve your problems.

8. Repeat

This step is the last and easiest step: Just repeat. When you find yourself overthinking, excessively worrying, or catch your negative thoughts attacking you again, go back to number one on this list. Start again. Do this every day and practice these steps fully with 100% of your effort put into it. If you do this right, you will notice a positive life and new surroundings developing within yourself. Slowly but surely, your old attitude and behaviors will disappear, making positivity your second nature.

STEP 6: HOW TO DECLUTTER YOUR MIND AND BECOME WHAT YOU WANT IN LIFE

A short brief of this chapter: You will learn how to get enough sleep, and stay asleep, so you have the energy to stay focused on being positive, developing self-confidence, improving your decision-making skills, stopping procrastination, starting to set goals, and learning more techniques on how to effectively solve problems. Perhaps this chapter is the most important chapter you have come across yet. So let's dive right in.

Insomnia

I want to start off with sleeping habits and what insomnia is because almost everything in this book, or what more there is to be read, involves getting enough sleep. You can't be productive if you don't have energy, so how can you tackle your mind traps when you are too tired to focus on them?

So, what is insomnia? Insomnia is when it becomes, or seems, impossible to get a good night's rest or even fall asleep. It may seem like your thoughts or other things in your life are keeping you awake at night, and so it's difficult to fall asleep. Some signs of insomnia are:

• Fatigue;

• Low energy (no matter what you do);

• It becomes challenging to focus on anything;

• Irritation or other mood changes;

• Decreased performance in work and school due to thought-patterns and lack of sleep.

There are different types of insomnia - let's take a look at them now:

Acute insomnia

This type of insomnia is situational. For instance, if you cannot sleep because of an exam you are dreading, a presentation you aren't completely prepared for, or an event you have been waiting months for.

Chronic insomnia

This is when your sleep is disrupted, meaning you cannot stay asleep once you have fallen asleep. This occurs at least three times a week and lasts for about three months or more.

Comorbid insomnia

This is a condition that is underlined by anxiety, depression, or other psychological conditions.

Onset insomnia

This is where you may have a difficult time falling asleep, no matter what the cause is.

Maintenance insomnia

This is when you can fall asleep, but you have a hard time staying asleep throughout the night. It then becomes difficult to fall back asleep.

Insomnia is not easy to live with, and it can disrupt many aspects of an individual's life. However, it is fixable with the right attitude and the proper motivation to do so.

How to Develop Better Sleep Habits

If the symptoms above sound about right, or if you have been diagnosed, then here are a few things that can help you sleep better:

1. Create a sleep routine

If you are not quite sure how to do this, then think about how you would put your baby, toddler, or children to sleep. Usually it starts about an hour before bed when you turn off technology, they get a bath, have a light snack and a glass of water, then it's pajama time, story time, and finally bedtime. Some kids may like it when you cuddle them or if you just rub their back or sing to them. Set up your own bedtime routine about an hour or so before you expect to sleep. By doing this regularly, and sticking to it, it will be easier for that mental noise to quiet down so you can unwind.

2. Exercise daily

Sometimes, the reason it is so challenging to fall asleep is because our bodies have too much energy. That restless leg syndrome is because your legs need to be stretched out and massaged. Whether you do it in the morning, or about two hours before you want to sleep, exercising is great to help the body relax itself later.

3. Limit technology

This is a big one because technology, like TV, phones, and other electronic devices, give off blue light that our brains detect as "daytime." This blue light makes our brains produce less melatonin (the chemical that promotes sleep), and our brains eventually don't know the difference between night and day. So turn off your technology - unless it's to listen to breathing exercises or guided meditations.

4. Make your bed for only sleeping or intimacy

It could be difficult to stay or fall asleep because you use your bed for practically everything. Do you eat on your bed? Visit friends on your bed? Do you talk on the phone in your bedroom? Is there a television set in your room? All these things can trick the brain into thinking your bed is more like a couch, and your room is more like a living room. When your mind interacts with your bed as a daily living area, it can be difficult for your mind to associate sleep with your bed. This can greatly increase insomnia symptoms. So take living out of your bedroom and start using other areas of your house for these daily activities instead.

5. Distract your mind with mental exercises before expecting to sleep

No, I don't mean use this as an excuse to go on your phone and play brain games. Go to the store and buy some pens, pencils, erasers, paper, and puzzle books. Or better yet, pick up a book from the store that you want to read. Get a magazine and read the comics or fill out the crossword puzzles. Pick up a scrabble board or single player card game and activate your mind with things you need to think about. Do some math or write in a journal. Yes, go old school and drop the technology. This not only distracts your mind from over-thinking, but also helps produce melatonin so that you find it easier to fall and stay asleep at night.

6. Practice relaxation methods

So this should be the only reason you use technology, unless you are willing to burn a CD full of relaxing music, beta wave audio playlists, and guided meditation videos. When you lay down to rest, breathe in through your nose and out through your mouth. Breathe with your stomach and gut, not your chest. This helps get more oxygen into your system and activates the brain to slow down and relax.

7. Heavy blankets

Heavy blankets are great for when you need that extra comfort. When we cuddle someone, we feel warmth and closeness. A heavy blanket acts like the same thing. So if you fall asleep with no problem, but then wake up throughout the night, then the heavy blanket is there as a safety net to get you back to sleep with little to no effort. A great idea if you suffer with maintenance insomnia is to put on relaxing music in the background for when you do sleep, so that when you wake up, the music will lull you back to sleep.

Hopefully these techniques help, and you will be able to stay asleep. It may not be immediate, but if you keep practicing these techniques, especially an hour or two before your bedtime, then sleep will come sooner rather than later. Along with these methods, make sure your "worry time" is way before you go to sleep. If you spend time worrying and going through your thoughts too close to when you plan on sleeping, then those thoughts can carry into your bedtime routine and make it more difficult to fall asleep because your brain will then learn that when it's time to sleep, it's time to think. We don't want that.

Decision-Making and Problem-Solving Techniques

It's a fact that you need effective decision-making skills to solve complicated or challenging problems. It's also a fact that in order to be an efficient problem solver, you need to understand that the decisions you make define the outcome of a solution. I have combined these two in one section because they are like two peas in a pod. Everything we learn on decision-making will tie into how you solve problems. If you need more help with problem solving, then the last chapter has very useful techniques on this topic.

Every skill has another skill that needs to be or can be learned. The skills needed to be effective in decision-making are:

• Processing the different decisions we can choose from for our set goal or outcome;

• Self-reflection or self-awareness;

• Creativity or analytical skills;

• Effective communication skills;

• Organizational skills.

These skills are needed so that we can reflect on our own attitudes and thoughts in order to make a decision and stick with them. Most times, people come up with multiple decisions that point to our official destination, so it is good to have organizational skills and creativity so that we can implement and pick them apart, leading us one step closer to the final decision.

The skills needed for effective problem-solving skills are:

• Creativity and logical reasoning skills;

• Research skills;

• Communication and socialization skills;

• Emotional intelligence;

• Decision-making.

Do you see a pattern? Almost all five of these skills somehow inter-relate to the decision-making process. Emotional intelligence is great to develop in both these skills as it allows you to think for yourself, reflect on attitudes, and feel empathy for other people. Emotional intelligence then leads to social intelligence, which is where you have good communication skills in getting what you want or need in a polite manner.

So, let's look deeper at what a problem is. A problem features goals and barriers. We have goals we want to reach, and then there are these hills or mountains, called barriers, that stand in our way to reach these goals. Problem solving is about overcoming these barriers so that we can reach our final destination: Our goals.

Problem-Solving Stages

In order to solve a problem, we must first go through the stages of that problem:

1. Identifying the problem

This is the stage where the problem arises. At this stage, the problem can be scattered and unclear so that it may seem really big, but when you think about and identify it, you can define what the actual problem is.

2. Researching for the problem

This is where we learn to observe and break down the problems revolving around the main problem. We look at the barriers, and we do some research on these barriers. When we do this, we develop a clearer picture of how we can fix the problem in our minds.

3. Searching for and making a list of solutions

After you have defined and broken down the problem and identified every barrier, you can then start finding possible solutions.

You can make a list of the outcomes based on your **creative skills** in finding a solution. Without evaluating too much, this is where our brains are in action to find a solution.

4. Making a decision

Once we have a list of solutions, it is time to make a decision. Using our **logical reasoning** or our **communication skills**, we can use these to pick the best solution in our previous step. Then when we make a decision, we stick with it and continue forward.

5. Taking action

This is the final stage where we have used all of our skills to make a final decision, and we put this decision into action. Moving forward, we don't look back; if we made a mistake, then we only learn from this later. Taking action is not to second-guess our decision or listen to the chatter in our minds that make us want to turn back. It is to overcome our fear that we had already done all we could and accept that this is what we will do now.

Basically, problem solving is just finding ways to solve a difficult or challenging task to reach our goal or destination. It's the decision-making process that defines how quickly we get over the barriers to solve these problems. Our minds usually get in the way with overthinking or second-guessing, and so this is why we need to learn how to make decisions without regretting them later.

How to Develop Decision-Making Skills

In this book, we have talked about shutting the mental chatter off, how to reboot the mind, and how to overcome our fears. The reason most people have a hard time with their decision-making skills is because they procrastinate implementing the solution, as they want to make sure it is the perfect decision that doesn't lead to failure. Failure is only implemented when you fear that you have not done your best, which stems from being a perfectionist, which also results in procrastinating with the decision-making process. One effective way to stop this spiral is to be confident in yourself that whatever decision you make, or are about to make, has been thoroughly researched and defined mentally or physically and that there is no other option. Be certain with your decisions and learn from them if they weren't what you expected. Positivity is the only outcome you should have in the end.

First, let's talk basics. Then, we will discuss other options for making these decisions while combining the basics with them:

Schedule a good thinking time

When you intentionally put aside some time in your day to think about the "problem" at hand, then you can figure out what your decisions around this problem might be.

Define your decisions

Just like defining the problem, you need to identify and lay out your decisions as well. Choose a number of decisions based on ONE problem at a time. When you have your decisions laid out, you can take a step back and determine which route is the best path to take.

Think through every option you choose

Every option you have come up with at this point needs to be properly thought out. Stop making more decisions because the more decisions you have, the more likely it will become a bigger piece of a pie you can't chew. The options you have now (limited to three to five) are the ones that need to be carefully thought out so you can solve your problem and reach your goal.

Now that the basics are covered, here are more things you can do involving the basics:

1. Ask yourself what your morals and values are

This is a big thing because it teaches us self-awareness and helps us perceive the decision-making process in a way we won't want to turn back from. Say you have two decisions in front of you: One could put your friend in a place where you may not be, and you would be sacrificing for their bene-fit; the other decision puts you on top and makes them your "sidekick." You need to pick one of these options based on what is going to make you the happiest. If it is seeing your friend in a better place than they are now because you have other ideas for yourself, then option one is better. However, if your friend is already in a good place and you need to be the one on top, then the second option is better. Whatever your core values are, don't stray from them because the "what if" games are never fun or helpful.

2. Imagine what the outcome will be

Close your eyes and picture what you imagine happening with the decisions you have outlined. Picture the best-case scenarios and the worst-case scenarios. Don't think too hard, and give yourself a five-minute time limit. Once that timer goes off, choose whatever decision you felt happiest about in the end.

3. Test it

In some cases, not all, this falls into play. For example, if your job is asking you to relocate, then go visit the city to which you have to move and see what your feelings are involved with this city. If you feel right, then go for it; if you feel off, then listen to that instinct and don't do it.

4. Listen to your hopes

Your hopes act like a compass for your gut instinct. It's your intuition shouting out at you to do something. So maybe your heart is one place and your mind is somewhere else. If you were to flip a coin, then what would you hope for it to be? If you were to ask someone for advice, then what would you hope for them to say? Whatever these instincts are, listen to them. If you make a decision based on defying these hopes, then you may not be happy with the results in the end and spend countless hours wishing you had picked the other option. Listen to your gut; most of the time, it's right.

Self-Confidence in Setting and Accomplishing Your Goals

Self-confidence is when you feel positively assured that you are correct in your judgements, abilities, power, values, and decisions, among other things. It is different from self-esteem in the fact that self-esteem is the evaluation of one's self-worth, but self-confidence is the ability to fully trust in ourselves to accomplish anything we set our minds to.

Some characteristics of a self-confident individual are:

• They do what they feel is right, even if someone else disagrees or criticizes them;

• They are determined to get what they want and go for it no matter what;

• They admit to their mistakes and take responsibility for their actions;

• They wait for acceptance or approval because they don't feel like they need to be praised;

• They do not boast or brag about their accomplishments;

• They willingly accept compliments;

• They feel comfortable being vulnerable;

• They don't feel the need to control or be jealous;

• They will not take blame if a relationship doesn't work out, nor do they blame the other person;

• They are confident that the decisions they make are good ones;

• They are self-aware and assertive.

All of these characteristics are perfect for making and maintaining goals and reaching your own potential. To be self-confident means that you are open to take risks and have little fear in the unknown because you are confident enough to accomplish what needs to be done.

Developing Self-Confidence

If these characteristics do not sound like you, then rest assured that they can be learned. If you don't develop or work on your self-confidence, then that is okay because you will still be able to get what you want; however, it may take longer, and your goals may be further away than you would like. It may seem like you are climbing a never-ending mountain of barriers to reach your desired destination. Some call this the way of life, but does life have to be this way? Here are some steps on how to develop and improve your self-confidence levels:

1. Step One: Formulating Your Adventure

There are five important things when it comes to getting yourself ready for self-confidence. These are explained below. To start your adventure, you must figure out where you are now, where you want to go, and believe in yourself that you can and will make this happen. You must develop the positivity and welcome this kind of commitment to change.

Look back at your achievements

When you think about your successes, try to name at least five things you have accomplished in your life thus far. Did you finish first in a marathon? Did you win at a hot dog eating contest? Were you an honor's student with A's in high school? Did you help a cat down from a tree? Or save a life? Whatever your achievements, big or small, they all count.

Notice your strengths

Once you have made your success list, you can then find out what your strengths are. Maybe for one of these achievements, you didn't do your best and you want to learn how to do better or more. When you notice your strengths, you can then move on to figuring out what your goals and barriers are surrounding these strengths. Ask yourself what you want to do. Where do you want to be? And who do you want to become? It is never too late to start this adventure.

Figure out what's most important to you

Setting and accomplishing goals is the number one thing surrounding your self-confidence. Self-confidence largely focuses on your ability to complete and strive towards your goals and continue to make new ones. The more accomplished you are, the more your self-confidence levels will improve. Even if you fail or make a mistake, confidence is about learning to grow from these mistakes and try harder the next time around. When you find out what's most important to you, you will realize that doing what you love is not that scary and failed attempts are part of the process.

Manage your mind

This book is all about managing your mind. You must practice positivity through this whole process. Challenge those negative thoughts, continue to reboot your brain, and work towards quieting those pesky worries. Combat your negative side and embrace your productive, positive side while continuing to strive for more confidence.

Commit to success

This final step to starting your adventure is perhaps the most important: You must promise yourself that no matter what, through thick and thin, you will commit to achieving your goals. You are basically making a vow to yourself to take steps forward every day to focus on your positivity, combating those unwanted thoughts, and becoming the best you can be. But wait, it's also more than that; it's believing that you **can** do this, and you **will**.

2. Step Two: Start Your Voyage

This step is where you set out on your voyage to complete your masterpiece. By this point, you should have completed a self-awarded measure of everything you have done. You should accept that your faults will continue, but you believe in yourself now. You should be able to say confidently and with pride that you are committed to becoming more because you value and appreciate yourself. Start with small, easy wins, and progress by completing bigger and bigger goals as you go forward. With every "win," make it a big deal and give yourself great rewards. This is how self-confidence will develop quicker.

Build knowledge

When you have made a list of your goals, look at them. Look at your strengths list and figure out what skills you will need to develop or learn to achieve these goals you have set. Once you have a set idea of how to achieve these goals, take a course and build knowledge around the steps to complete your goal. Strive for certifications and become qualified for what you want to accomplish.

Concentrate on the basics

Do small things, but do them well. Don't reach for perfection, just implement change and focus on the basics. When you are just starting out, you do not want to overwhelm yourself with elaborate or crafty goals that are just out of your reach. This will come later.

Set small goals and complete them

Follow this routine in the beginning: Set a goal, accomplish it, celebrate your success, and move on to something a little more difficult than the previous goal. The goal within this step is to get in the habit of setting goals and accomplishing them. Only over time will your goals get bigger and bigger, but the trick is that you do it so gradually that, by the time you get to your furthest goal you have been working towards, you won't notice the increasing difference in difficulty.

Continue working on your mind

Continue to stay on top of challenging those negative thoughts and overthinking chatter in your mind. Continue to progress with positivity and let go of the fears around uncertainty.

3. Step Three: Strive Forward Towards Success - Take Action

This is where you take action to complete every step before this one. This is the step that sets you up for all your successes. You are done figuring out your adventure here, you have completed your voyage quest, and now you are ready to implement all the data you found along the way. Here is where you take action for completing more difficult and prolonged goals. With every accomplished goal, you get higher rewards and more fulfillment. When you have reached your desired goal – such as maybe owning a large property and being manager of a corporate business - you can celebrate all your past achievements and be confident that you will succeed in anything else you do because you have been doing it the whole time. Self-confidence is not something you grow overnight, but something that, in a few years from now (maybe even weeks or months), you can say you are more confident today than the day you started this adventure.

Changing Your Relationships with People

Many times, the reason for our inner negativity is because of the people we surround ourselves with. Overthinking is influenced by our decisions and what our company tells us. It is time to make decisions for ourselves now that we have learned how to be more confident in making these wiser choices.

Here are some points on how to identify a negative person in your life:

• They are worry-warts;

- They are opinionated about your life;

- They are secretive;

- They view the world pessimistically;

- They are sensitive to your suggestions and anything you tell them;

- They are master complainers;

- They favor the word "but";

- They don't try hard to fix themselves or their lives;

- They make excuses;

- They suck your energy from you;

- They see the dark side of every positive thing;

- They are selfish.

Dealing with a Negative Person

Your happiness may be caused by the relationships you have and the company you keep. When you're dealing with negative people, your positive vibes may start to decrease, and then you are back into the same habits as you were before you grabbed this book. Humans are social creatures, so it makes sense as to why so many of us are sponges to other's behaviors. While we try hard not to upset the ones we love, other times we are unsure about if we did something wrong to upset them. Of course, not everyone can get along, but we sure try.

Dealing with a negative person can be quite difficult, but here is the key point to managing them: You cannot control them; you can only control how you act as a result of being around them. If you can fix, mend, or continue with this person by setting boundaries and being assertive, then do so. If you can't and every interaction with them seems to just drag you down despite your efforts, then it is best to get rid of them entirely or decrease how much you talk to them.

Here are a few healthy ways of dealing with negative or toxic relationships:

• **Set positive boundaries**

Negative people don't recognize when they are being negative or even consider anyone's feelings as a result of their negativity. When you are interacting with a toxic person, consider setting boundaries internally and outwardly. Tell yourself that you will not allow them to make you feel bad. If your mood or your thoughts start to change when being around this person, you need to walk away. Kindly tell them that you will not engage in this conversation if they cannot learn to be more positive, and then politely walk away.

Another thing you can do is start the interaction. Be pumped and make them feel positive before discussing anything with them. When you tell a negative person to act positive, they feel judged, whereas if you act positive and make them feel positivity, then your vibe can make them feel lighter and they will return that positivity throughout your interaction. This may result in closeness and less conflict.

• Question the worth of this friendship or relationship

You need to ask yourself a few questions about your relationships. Try writing down all the people you know and want to know more. Then, ask yourself: "Who is this person to me? What is my relationship like with them? Are they negative? How often do you hang out just because, or is it because they need something from you?" The answers to these questions may seem surprising, or maybe not. However, the answers will help you identify if the relationship is worth taking care of or if it may be best to just walk away from them entirely.

• Don't take it personally, even if it seems personal

Anything that a negative person says to you could be because they had a bad day, they have their own opinions, they are judgmental, or they feel like they are trying to help you by giving you advice. However, you should determine their intent behind the advice they give and the way you feel about your conversation. When they advise you to do something, is it coming from the fact that they care deeply about your needs, or is it because it is their opinion about what you should or shouldn't do? A positive person takes things that others say lightly because they are confident in themselves to do what's right for them. Regardless of their tone, pay more attention to the words they are saying so that you can address the meaning behind them.

• Act, don't react

When we look at the list we created, we may already have a sense of the individuals who struggle with positivity. Knowing this already, the next time you are faced with this individual, willfully create positive feelings and don't wait for an opportunity. Give them a compliment or boost their spirits by telling them what you admire about them. This may give them relief and set the ball rolling for what they can expect from you.

• Determine the reality of the relationship

Many times, we perceive things our own way and then try to get others to think the way we do. We offer our advice and when they don't take it, we may feel disbelief, which can make us angry or unsettled. When addressing a negative person, think about the reality of your relationship and their own reality. Why are they negative? What can you do to help them be positive and keep your sanity? This means that after you have done all that, you can take a break. Take these negative people in short doses and change your perspective about the reality of the bond. Start by telling yourself, "All I can do for my friend is love them for who they are. I will help them when they need it, but if they don't want to accept change, then I need to do what is best for myself as well as be understanding of their needs."

• You are not a problem solver

The saying goes, *"You cannot help someone who does not want to be helped."*[1] Instead of wasting your energy to help a negative person if they don't want to make change, sometimes you may just have to accept this. Overcoming excessive worrying is about letting go of what you cannot control. So, when your negative company continues to be negative, remind yourself that you are not their friend to solve their problems. You are their friend because you choose to be there for them. If there is a time where you need to walk away for good, then this is what you may need to do. Don't feel guilty.

Changing Your Relationship with Your Spouse

Aside from toxic negativity with the company you keep, having a toxic spouse can be even worse for your negative thought-patterns. Relationships are hard, and they take work, but a relationship is not always toxic because both of you are unhealthy, sometimes it's only one of you. A toxic person – or spouse – may not know that they are toxic or negative because they are too self-absorbed with their own needs, wants, frustrations, goals, and interests to worry about yours.

Here are a few questions to ask yourself to identify if you are in an unhealthy relationship:

• How do you feel when you are with this person?

• Do you feel safe when you are near this person?

• How does your spouse affect your children and your life?

• Do you feel emotionally stressed-out or exhausted when you are with them?

• Are you more tense when you are with them?

• Is this person manipulative or deceitful?

• When you are with them, compared to when you are not, how do you feel?

• Is life more challenging than it needs to be when you are together?

• Do you find yourself changing for the needs of your spouse?

These answers can greatly challenge your thoughts and help you decide on what you should do next. Most people stay in relationships because they are gaining something out of their partner. This includes things like affection, intimacy, money, power, children, what you have built together, love, and the inability to see negative changes. We stay because we get stuck in the thought that things will change, or if we do this, then this will happen. Regardless of the reasons for staying, we need to sit with ourselves and determine whether it is worth it for our health to stay or leave.

Changing Your Relationship for the Better

If you have chosen to give it another shot, then there are a few things that you may not have done yet. If the following list doesn't work out very well, then professional therapy may be the better route to go. However, you need to determine how much energy is healthy to put your efforts into because it takes two to make a relationship healthy again. You both need to commit to getting to know each other again (as people change over years) and spend more time working on discipline, compromise, motivation, and desire. If these aspects are gone, then there are ways you can get them back with the power of positivity. Commit to doing something together everyday to restore respect and love back into your relationship.

Here are a few tips to help get you back on track or "change" your existing relationship:

1. Talk to your spouse

Telling your spouse exactly what you need, what the problem is, and then coming together to fix these worries is crucial for staying on track. When you have been with someone for a while, you start to know their habits, their routine, and their way of life. However, we forget to discuss our concerns which usually ends in arguing or disagreements. When you talk, make sure to use calm voices and a low tone. Try not to nag about your worries but use positivity all the way through.

2. Communicate with "I" statements

A lot of the time, we fall into "you" statements, such as, "You aren't doing enough," or, "You make me do these things as retaliation." One thing to get clear is that your partner is never responsible for your thoughts or actions. You think for yourself, and "you" statements can come off as blaming or bullying. To avoid this hostility, practice "I" statements, such as, "I feel hurt because…" or, "I am upset because…" When you tell your spouse how they are making you feel, then in the same sentence, also tell them what they can do to change it. For example, "I feel disrespected when you don't call me when you are out; next time, I would like it if you could give me a call and answer my messages."

3. Be consistent

Problems need to be talked about and then addressed with solutions. Once you have created clear boundaries and new "rules" for your relationship, stick to them. If your spouse has disrespected you, then remind them of these conversations and ask them to remind you of the same if you fall off track. Changing your relationship is a team effort and it will take work to become healthy again.

4. Be who you are and the best version of self

You cannot focus on a relationship and the demanding needs it asks of you if you are not managing your own wants, needs, and emotions. So, while you practice all the techniques in this book, implement them into every conversation so that you can be a happier, healthier you. Don't settle for less than what you know you can be, even when it comes to people you love.

5. Spend needed time together

Relationships are not just about arguments and learning about each other as we go; they're more than that. Sure, you are going to bicker and have disagreements, but the more you spend non-argumentative quality time together the healthier your relationship can become, even in those dark times. Quality time is about putting distractions away, like your phone, and talking one-on-one with each other. Play a card game, sit in front of the fire, or go for an evening stroll. Do things you have wanted to do and re-spark your relationship by doing what you haven't done in a while or reminiscing about what happened when you first got together.

6. Touch is essential

Along with quality time, touch is also essential. It has been proven from multiple studies that physical touch releases those endorphins needed to make you happy. To welcome touch into your relationship, start by holding their hand in public or brushing their shoulder or back when you pass by them. The next step is to cuddle on the couch (without intercourse). The power of physical touch without sexual intercourse speaks great lengths for the positivity of any relationship. When the moment is right, go one step further and make touching more sexual.

7. Learn the power of communication

Everything we do revolves around communication. When we argue, our moods become sour; when we laugh, our moods become happier. The way we talk, listen, and respond all has to with whether we will feel positive or negative vibes at the end of our conversations. Sometimes, it's better not to say anything at all, and the sound of silence can speak volumes. Pick up some communication books or talk to a professional and learn ways to communicate with your spouse, and vice versa.

8. Stay true to yourself and your values

No matter who someone is, they should never make you second guess what is most important to you. Write down a list of the absolute things that cannot and will not be negotiable, and then the things that are "maybes." On this list, see what your core values are and make sure your spouse knows that these things are important boundaries. This is how you can stay true to yourself and know whether or not to walk away if they are uncompromisable.

9. Listen to your partner

One thing you will learn in communication courses is that listening is half the battle. When you listen to your partner's needs and wants, listen with your full attention. This means turn off all distractions, like music, television, noises outside, etc. Make sure that when you have a conversation you go somewhere quiet and it isn't in the middle of a busy day. That way you can hear and try to comprehend what your partner is telling you. Listening is an effective and necessary step to communicate well.

10. Communicate your wants

Once you have identified where the relationship has fallen apart (or if it is on its way), it is essential to communicate what you want to your spouse. Ask for what they would like to see, and then tell them what you would like to happen more. No one can read anyone's mind, so communicating your wants to your spouse can greatly improve your relationship. Maybe they have been holding something in for a while, and if you are open to hearing what they need to say non-judgmentally, then you can learn to understand how to work together.

STEP 7: SIMPLE DAILY PRACTICES TO OVERCOME PROCRASTINATION

When talking about procrastination, everyone might relate to it because there isn't anyone who could deny it. At least, once or twice in your life, procrastination would have played its role. Whenever you miss your deadlines, the level of anxiety rises above your head and you are forced to complete the project as soon as possible. But deep down, you know it is impossible to complete because there is so much to do. Yet, you try! Procrastination will make your life miserable, so try not to make it a habit.

Some people want to stop procrastinating, but they are unable to because they don't know how to do it. Or sometimes, they might be missing the motivation they need. And it can be frustrating, I know. You must understand the fact that procrastinating factors differ from one individual to another:

A writer will procrastinate on the project he/she was assigned. And then, he/she must work day and night to complete the project.

A student will delay school work and then, complete it at the last moment.

An athlete will delay medications because they are so concerned about the current game.

If you evaluate each example above, you will understand that through procrastination every individual mentioned in the example will be affected. For instance, the athlete will have to deal with a lot of severe issues if he/she doesn't treat the injury right away. Likewise, there will be a lot of emotional drawbacks as well.

I am going to share some of the practical daily practices that you can follow to overcome procrastination. These practices will help you beat procrastination even if you are feeling lazy or unmotivated. Before you begin reading the practices below, you must bear in mind that you can select any of them. This means you are not forced to perform all the habits below. Let's get started!

1. Find solutions to potential emergencies

Procrastination is not just simply a bad habit; rather it is a dangerous one. It will have a huge impact on your health. Sometimes, you might even lose the great bonds that you shared with your family members. They might even come to a point where they assume that you no longer care. There will be situations in life where you have to deal with unexpected priorities such as death, sickness, and much more. Such situations can't wait because you will have to address them immediately. In such an instance, you would have to drop all the scheduled tasks. Some other times, great family events might turn into dreadful situations, and you can't avoid them and get back to your work. Emergencies don't come with a warning, so you have to put up with the obstacles they create. How can you avoid emergencies? Are you going to stop everything and address the issue? Or if you have already delayed the work and then, something urgent comes up, how are you planning to handle it? What might happen when you ignore the emergencies?

To handle emergencies, you have to have a clear picture of the type of emergencies that you are dealing with. You can think about the aftereffects of avoiding the emergency. Or think about the people who are related to the emergency, how will they feel if you ignore it? What are the actions that you can take to solve this sudden issue so that you can get back to work? Or can you put off the emergency issue because it is not life-threatening?

Before you dig in further, let me tell you. If you are working so hard that you don't even have time for your family, it means you are losing a lot of good things in life, there is a lack of balance. You are not living your life — this where the concept of smart working comes into the picture. You can easily get busy and forget about the people around you. Or you can easily put off emergencies that you believe are not important, and those emergencies might actually turn into severe situations. Of course, you might be so busy that you don't even have time for important things, but it is all about your priorities.

No project, appointment, or meeting is worth ignoring for the emergencies that might affect the life of a loved one. I'd suggest stopping other things when something urgent comes up because procrastination is not only about work but also about life. If you address emergencies right away, you won't have to deal with the worst cases down the line.

Most of the time, we think procrastination is all about work and how we delay work. But I hope I have pointed out something that you should also consider.

If you organize work-related activities and complete them before the deadline, or if you have completed half the work already, unexpected priorities might not create a huge impact on your work life. What matters is being organized and knowing how to prioritize your life matters.

2. Carry out daily reviews

Another excellent way to avoid procrastination is through daily reviews. If you allocate ten minutes from your day, you can assess how things are going. When you are doing the review, you will be able to find the priorities of your day. Then, you can analyze the tasks that will have a huge impact on your short-term goals. To make this review session simpler, consider carrying out a Q&A format. What are the scheduled meetings that you need to attend? Are there any emails that you must reply to today? Are there any documents that need to be edited today? Are there any appointments that will take more time than you allocated? What are the tasks that require more attention?

Likewise, you should do a Q&A to find out the layout of the day. But you don't have to stick to the questions that I have mentioned. Instead, you can prepare your own Q&A and follow it. If you do this daily review, you will be able to understand the layout for the day. When you have your layout, you will be able to stay on the track. You will have proper knowledge of the tasks that need more time or a quick response. Hence, you will not procrastinate because you are aware that it will impact your goals negatively.

If you want to know one of the best concepts that beat procrastination, it is the Pareto Principle. This is all about an 80/20 rule. Try to learn more about this concept before you apply it to your day-to-day activities.

3. MIT's or the Most Important Tasks

It's tough to beat procrastination if you begin your day with a to-do-list that bursts with tasks. You must have a simplified to-do-list if you want to get things done on time and correctly. How can you simplify your to-do-list? It is pretty simple if you focus on MIT's - most important tasks. You have to settle for the tasks that will have a considerable impact on your long-term goals. This is recommended by many experts who focus on productivity.

My tips are to select the top three important tasks that need to be handled by the end of the day. It is better to pick two important tasks that have tight deadlines and another that will impact your long-term career goal. If you keep an eye on MIT's concept, you will be able to curb procrastination. Once you complete the two most important activities, you will be interested in doing the other activities by the end of the day. And that motivation is very much needed if you want to succeed in beating procrastination.

4. The Eisenhower Matrix

Who doesn't like productivity? Who isn't glad when things happen the way they were planned. But sometimes, things don't work as you planned. If your life is anything like mine, filled with constant emergencies and changes, you must have the ability to make quick decisions.

If you want to make a quick decision, you need the support from the Eisenhower Matrix. The founder of this concept, Dwight Davis Eisenhower, was a general in the army. It was the reason why he invented this concept. It's not always possible to work according to the plan when you are in an army. There will be sudden and important changes. In such an instance, the Eisenhower Matrix concept was the guideline.

If Eisenhower utilized this in the army, there is no reason why we can't utilize this in our lives to avoid procrastination! When you are dealing with this concept, you shouldn't forget the four quadrants related to it. By focusing on the four quadrants, you will be able to approach your day-to-day tasks accordingly. Let me mention the four quadrants in detail:

Quadrant 1: Urgent plus important

These are the tasks that need to be completed first because they are way more important than any other tasks and they directly deal with your career goals. Plus, you must complete the tasks right away because they are urgent. If you complete these tasks, you will be able to avoid negative consequences. Once you get your Q1 tasks completed, you will be able to focus on other tasks. For example, if you have to submit a project by the end of the day, your complete attention should be given to that project because it is both urgent and important.

Quadrant 2: Important yet not urgent

The tasks under Q2 are important, but they are not urgent. Even though they might have a huge impact, they are not as time-sensitive as Q1. Compare Q2 to Q1, and then, you will understand the difference clearly. Typically, Q2 tasks will include the ones that have a huge impact on your long-term career or life goals. Yes, you need to allocate more time and attention to these tasks. But you seldom do it because your mind knows that the tasks in Q2 can wait.

Meanwhile, you'll be focused on the tasks in other quadrants. Don't make this mistake because your long-term goals are the reasons why your short-term goals exist. For example, your health is one of the important factors, so if you don't spend enough time on it, you will regret it. Yet, when you get busy, you are unlikely to spend time on Q2 tasks. Especially, you are not obliged to answer to anyone about Q2 tasks.

Quadrant 3: Urgent yet not important

The tasks under Q3 are urgent, but you don't necessarily have to spend your time on them. You can either automate or delegate tasks to someone who can handle the work. These tasks are not so important, so it is okay to delegate them. These tasks often come from a third party and the tasks under Q3 will not have a direct influence on your career goals. But when you are handling Q3 tasks, you must note down the tasks that you delegate. For example, if you are working on a time-sensitive project and the phone rings, you might get distracted answering it. Or sometimes, it might not even be an important call. For such activities, you can assign someone. Even if it's an urgent call, you can still assign it to a person who can handle it. Through this, you will be able to manage your day!

Quadrant 4: Not important plus not urgent

The tasks under Q4 include the tasks that need to be avoided. These tasks waste your time unnecessarily. If you don't spend ANY time on Q4 tasks, you will be able to spend more time on the tasks under Q2. By now, you'll know what Q4 tasks consist of. Anyway, they are activities like watching TV, surfing the Internet, playing games, and much more. So, should you eliminate Q4? Well, no! You shouldn't. If you don't have a balanced lifestyle, you might even struggle to protect your job. The tasks in Q4 will help you whenever you take a 5-minute break or whenever you want to step away from work. These tasks shouldn't even be in your mind when you are trying to be productive.

To apply the Eisenhower Matrix to your life, start by drawing a table on a piece of paper or your journal. Then, divide the table into four columns and seven rows. Divide the rows according to the days and add the quadrants to the columns. When your table is ready, analyze your week. But don't write anything down yet. Before you start the day, think, analyze again and allocate the tasks as per the matrix. If something else comes up, you must take some time to analyze the nature of the task, and then classify it in the right quadrant.

Once you complete all seven days, you can study the table and evaluate your effectiveness and productivity. This will not be amazing when you try it for the first time, but don't give up. Keep trying, and eventually, you will find yourself spending more time on the important and urgent tasks.

If you keep following this technique, you will be able to structure your day-to-day tasks, and it will help your success become better and better!

5. Do it quickly

Sometimes you come across tasks that don't need a lot of time, not even five minutes, yet you delay it. For example, cleaning after having dinner, sending an email, or even changing into your PJs (this is laziness). Even though these tasks don't take much time, you don't do them because you consider yourself too busy.

Your way of ignoring quick or minor tasks is by telling yourself you have too much to do. But the problem is whenever you delay minor tasks, it builds up into a pile, and you might have to deal with huge tasks at the end. If you don't act immediately, you will have a lot to do when you take days off. Also, if you complete the minor tasks quickly, you will be able to avoid them from accumulating into bigger tasks. There are two practices that you should consider if you want to get minor tasks done.

The Two-Minute Rule is one of the practices that you must follow. If you think that the task will only take two minutes or less, you can do it instead of putting it off, can't you? So whenever you come across any minor tasks, think whether it will take longer to finish those. If they don't, why not get them done? Also, if you follow this habit throughout, you will feel that you are removing a lot of negativity and you have more time to spend on important tasks. Besides, you'll feel that you are more organized and than you have achieved more than before.

In contradiction, if you find tasks that will need more than five minutes, you must schedule a time to do it.

The second practice is to single-handle all the possible tasks. Let me describe an example, say that you've received an email and even though it requires a reply, you delay answering it. But then, when you check it later, you would have forgotten the details on the email itself and so you have to go through the whole thing again. Instead of making this simple task a huge pain, you can easily get it done. The concept of single handling helps you complete the tasks. If you can see the end clearly, you must make the necessary actions. For example, you can do the dishes right away instead of putting it off for later. Likewise, there are many short tasks that you have to complete immediately.

If you follow these concepts, you will be able to complete minor tasks quickly and overcome procrastination. In fact, the stress that tags along with procrastination can also be eliminated completely.

These are the simple practices that will help you beat

procrastination. You don't have to worry or think badly about yourself just because you are a procrastinator. We all have been procrastinators at some point in our lives. Everyone can beat procrastination if they try! Now, you have many practical tips that you can follow. You can utilize them and see if there are any changes!

You are way more powerful than you think, so ONLY you can decide whether to become a procrastinator or a productive individual!

TROUBLESHOOTING GUIDE (IF NOTHING HELPS)

This is a short chapter to summarize and implement what we have learned in this book, aside from the conclusion. This chapter is a short guide to help you for when you fall off track and need some assistance on those dark and challenging days.

Get Back on Track

Let's say you did everything, you practiced the techniques in this book, and then out of nowhere everything seems to be falling apart. Your negative thought-patterns came back, you have started to worry and overthink everything again, and you just need a quick pick me up - Here is how to get back on track in three easy steps:

1. Identify the problem, and find the root cause

Usually, when we try to do something new, our old habits try to sneak their ways back into our lives, making it that much more difficult to continue changing our habits. This is because we haven't found the root of our problem. Try to re-identify the root of the problem by addressing your triggers. Here are some trigger examples that may be causing you to fall off track:

• Stress from changes and relationships;

• Boredom from lack of progress;

• Chronic illness or injury;

• Change in environment, like moving or vacationing;

• Doing too much too soon.

To avoid your old habits creeping up on you, take some "me time" to figure out what triggered you to fail in the first place. Don't look at this as failure, but as a chance to start again with more knowledge.

2. Restart the behavior by practicing your positive-habit training

Go back to the basics and remind yourself that overthinking is not going to do anything but make you counterproductive. Don't ignore your thoughts, instead acknowledge them and practice mindfulness that they are there. Set a worry schedule and write your worries down to deal with during this time of worry. Practice meditation, and if you have been lacking, then dedicate yourself to some exercise. By doing these things slowly, it will force your brain to remember the habits you were trying to form and get you back on track to challenging your thought-patterns. When you have this down pat again, go back and make small goals and reward yourself when you accomplish them.

3. Try a different approach

Not all methods of action work for everyone, so find a different approach that suits you better. For example, if your worry time is right after dinner, around 6pm, start your worry time before dinner, around 3pm. Or maybe you woke up, started working out, then showered after that, but you fail because you find you're rushing your day due to this routine. So work out just before you wind down for sleep. By finding a different approach, you may just find something that works best with your schedule, then getting on track will come easily.

Calm Anxiety (Worrying) in Five Minutes or Less

Anxiety and other mood disorders are common for enabling your old habits to return to the surface. This is because our anxieties allow us to do what is familiar and "safe." Anxiety doesn't like change and it will seem as though you are constantly having to restart because you give into your anxieties and fall back rather than shoot forward. The trick to overcoming this is figuring out ways to calm down immediately. Here are ways to do just that:

1. Play the 5-5-5 game

The 5-5-5 game is a grounding technique. Look around the

room and name five things you can see. Close your eyes, take in a deep breath and name five things you can hear. Keep your eyes closed, or re-open them, move five body parts, and name them. (For example, move your wrists and say aloud "wrist," move your toes and say aloud "toes.") Start again and do this as many times as you can until you feel calm. Be completely in the present as if you are seeing, hearing, and moving for the first time.

2. Do a quick exercise   Jumpin Jacks

Jump up and down, spin in circles, stretch, pace, move the muscles in your face, wiggle every part of your body, dance, or any activity to get your body moving.

Do anything you can do for exercise, maybe go for a light jog or a brisk walk to change your surroundings.

Sometimes all your body needs is a little exercise to get past the initial adrenaline rush of anxiety. While you are exercising, pay attention to the weak feeling in your legs or the tingle in your fingertips. Move past this, and this trains your brain to overcome these uncomfortable feelings healthily.

3. Throw a cold cloth on your neck

By putting a cold cloth on your neck, holding an ice cube, or taking a cold shower, you are shocking the anxiety out of your system. Sometimes all your body needs is a quick shock to bring your attention away from the anxiety or worried thoughts.

4. Eat a lemon or a banana

Taste buds are a quick way to shock your system too. Eating a lemon will make your face scrunch and your body jolt, and so the worries or overthinking which are causing the anxiety will instantly stop. Bananas hold a ton of nutrients that will bring your sugar levels back to normal as well. Sometimes you may just be having a sugar attack from high or low sugar intake, so a banana will bring these levels back to normal, which will make you feel calmer.

5. Question your anxiety

Take a minute before you panic to address your thoughts. Question them. What is causing the anxiety? Which of the cognitive distortions do these thoughts fall under? Are you underestimating your ability to handle this right now? Is this a false alarm? What can you do about it? What is the worst that can happen? When you stop to answer these questions in full, you will notice that your mind doesn't have the attention span to send negative symptoms to your body and think about how to answer these questions at the same time. This may make you feel calmer. When these questions are answered, take a minute to focus on your breathing, sit down, and be mindful of your breaths.

Quick Methods to Decrease Negative Thinking

On those days where your thought-patterns have drowned out all the positive, and you find yourself falling into the mindless chatter surrounded by negative thinking, follow these easy methods to get out of it quickly:

1. Cut it off

This technique requires you to act quickly. The second you realize you are thinking negative thoughts, cut them off. Yell "STOP" inside your mind, or even out loud. Don't pay attention to the negative thinking, don't argue, defend yourself, or analyze it. Just cut it off as if it doesn't exist. Immediately think about something else or get up and do something else. Find a distraction so that you are no longer listening to your negative thoughts.

2. Label the thoughts

If cutting them off doesn't work, then try labelling them. Acknowledge that what you are thinking is negative, remind yourself that it is only a thought. You can choose to pay attention to it or ignore it, either way you don't have to act on it as it is only a thought and it does not define your actions. Negative thoughts only have power over you if you give them the control to dictate your actions. It isn't about how we challenge our thoughts, but how we react to them. When we do nothing about them, we gain our control back. So repeat to yourself, "This is only a negative thought, and I don't have to do anything about it."

3. Exaggerate the thoughts

Another way to take control of your negative thinking is to simply exaggerate the original thought. For example, imagine you are trying to learn something, and you just don't get it. You have been at it for hours and you notice yourself thinking, "There is no point in trying, I am just stupid and will never learn." Acknowledge that this is negative, and then exaggerate it outrageously and make it humorous. So say, "Yes; in fact, I am so stupid that I couldn't even screw in a lightbulb if I tried. And because I am this dumb, everyone will notice, so they will laugh at me. After they are finished laughing, I will give them a reason to laugh and start hopping around like a kangaroo, yelling like a donkey, to the point where everyone, including myself, will laugh. Then after that, I will show myself just how silly stupid I can be." Continue like this, using your imagination and being as sarcastic as you can, not taking anything you purposely say personal. When you do this, I bet you your mind will be quiet after this.

4. Counteract

This technique is the opposite of the last technique. When your mind says, "I am so stupid," say the exact opposite and nothing more. So that would look like, "I am the smartest person in this room." If your mind says, "I will never be good enough," then say, "I will always be good enough." When your mind says, "I'm too stupid to understand this stuff," say, "I am too smart to understand this stuff." This works because when we think too much about our negative thoughts, we usually fear ourselves acting them out. And when we fear acting upon them, the fear usually comes true because we end up doing what we try so hard not to do because we give it too much attention. So when we say the opposite to our thoughts, we aren't really paying attention to them, rather we are forcing our minds to think positively.

5. Enforce positive affirmations

For every negative thought, come up with two positive affirmations. So when your mind says, "I am not good enough," say, " I am grateful to be enough for the world today," and, "It's a good thing I am beautiful, because this negative thought could really get the best of me if I let it." The reason we come up with two positive affirmations for every one negative thought is to be more focused on positive thinking than negative thinking. Over the course of your day, you may feel so good about yourself that you give yourself credit for making yourself feel this way.

CONCLUSION

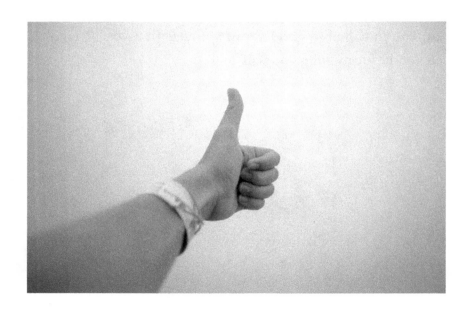

I hope you enjoyed reading my book on how to stop mental chatter. The techniques revolving around negative thinking, overthinking, and excessive worrying have been thoroughly

researched, and I promise all the information in this b
completely true. The techniques that are given to you to
throughout this book have been discussed and explained by
many professionals and tried by many people. They are
effective and will work when you put your mind, body, and
soul into them.

My hopes for this point forward in your life is to continue to
practice the positive techniques and really develop the ways
of avoiding negative thinking and unreasonable worrying.
The only advice I have left is, now that you have finished
reading, go back and highlight your favorite parts of this
book or fold the corner of the page so you can come back
when you are in need. That way, when you catch yourself
falling backwards after trying to take steps forward, you can
easily go back to where in this book that helped you the
most and fix the problem.

Good luck in your future successes and stay healthy

Cheers!

SOME BOOKS YOU MAY FIND INTERESTING

How to Stop Procrastinating

A Proven Guide to Overcome Procrastination, Cure Laziness & Perfectionism, Using Simple 5-Minute Practices

Do you struggle with procrastination and laziness? Have no free time for your loved one, your family, your friends? Think that you are missing your life, limiting your potential? Feel overwhelmed and guilty about yourself and beloved people?

If you want to stop it once and for all, then keep reading.

There is no counter argument whether or not procrastination kills your productivity. It indeed kills your productivity. For example, if you have been given a week to complete a project, you must use it in the best way to get your work done. Instead, you may spend your time scrolling through Facebook feeds, Instagram, Twitter, or watching Netflix.

When you are nearing the deadline, you might have to run a race to achieve your goal, and it will have a huge black spot on the quality.

Sometimes, by the time you understand the influence caused by procrastination, it will be too late to correct things. In life, you have to seize the chances that you get because it only takes a few seconds before it reaches another person.

But I would like to share something interesting; some people get the work done with quality even if they get it done in a short time due to procrastinating. Yes, such people do exist, and we'll discuss their habits and tips in this book.

Yes, procrastination is more dangerous than many of us assume. However, there are always solutions for all problems. Even for procrastination, you have many practical solutions that can be practiced with perseverance and diligence.

What you'll learn:

• 27 Tactics to Beat Your Procrastination.

• Simple Daily Practices, Tools and Apps to Stop Procrastinating for Good.

• How to Cure Laziness and Break Lazy Habits.

• How to Deal with Perfectionism.

• 10 Tips and Tricks to Get Things Done in Less Time.

• One Powerful Technique to Get Everything That You Want in Life

Even if there are distractions, you must be able to focus on the important things. If you know how to differentiate important tasks and trivial tasks, you'd easily overcome procrastination.

But the difficulty is in taming your mind. For this, we'll discuss many practical tips and exercises. So this book will help you make time for the ones who actually need it.

Would You Like To Know More?

Download this book to get started, and stop procrastinating for good!

Mind Hacking Secrets

21 Neuroscience Ways to Develop Fast, Clear & Critical Thinking. Learn How to Train Your Brain to Think Faster and Clearly in 2 Weeks.

Do you long to be able to have clear thinking, a clear mind, organizational skills, and the ability to recall information more efficiently? Are there moments when you wish you could learn faster, remember more, and be more productive?

Your brain is an incredible tool that will never fail to amaze even the most talented scientists out there, but...

The problem is that it isn't thinking in the way that you want it to. You can get hung up on small details, become easily distracted, and forget important information that you want to remember.

The solution to your biggest neuroscience issues lies within your head. There is no pill, surgery, or another quick method that is going to give you a new way of thinking. All the changes that you wish to make within your neurology are entirely possible by using your brain!

We are going to give you actionable steps to help you get the results you want.

This book is going to be a practical guide for you to improve the way that you think overall. The purpose of this reading will be to provide you with foundational "how-to" knowledge so you can apply what you learn to your life to see instant results.

We will teach you how to think fast, clearly, and critically.

We will help you improve your focus, reasoning, judgment, analysis, and ability to make certain choices. We will help you increase your writing skills, as well as your ability to speak.

You will understand how to keep your brain sharp through critical thinking, improved decision-making skills, and problem-solving abilities. When you practice applying these methods and practical tips that are discussed throughout this book, you are unlocking your greatest potential.

What you'll learn:

• How to Be More Productive and Do More in a Less Time.

• 21 Neuroscience Ways to Develop Fast, Clear and Critical Thinking.

• How to Hack Your Way to a Sharper, Smarter, and More Resilient Brain.

• Powerful Methods for Developing Critical Thinking and Avoiding Manipulation Tactics

• Action Plan for How to Train Your Brain to Think Faster in 2 Weeks

We will provide you with all that is needed to unlock the secrets of your mind. This is a must-read for anyone that wants to know how they can get the things they desire most with the full use of their brain.

Would you like to know more?

Get your copy now and start training!

package
help

Unlimited Memory Power

How to Remember More, Improve Your Concentration and Develop a Photographic Memory in 2 Weeks.

Do you want to have a better memory? Do you want to boost your brain so you can learn faster, remember more, and be more productive?

Perhaps you want to have a photographic memory and want to be a superhero who can remember all kinds of information, including details of facts, people's names, and events...

We have everything you need in this book, *Unlimited Memory Power*. As you read, you will learn actionable steps to get the results you want by improving memory and boosting your memory's capacity. You will discover how to train your brain to remember more and learn faster, using special memory improvement exercises.

This book presents a plan to train your memory with a challenge for your mind, body, and soul. We offer a total

— diet, exercise, stress relief, and memory tricks to you remember.

In this book, you will learn basic skills and more advanced strategies, including mnemonic devices, the memory palace, the military method, and much more.

You will train a photographic memory that enables you to remember faces and names, numbers, dates, foreign languages, and even game cards. I will also show you how to improve your reading skills. Also, we will talk about the foods that contribute to your memory.

What you'll learn:

• Advanced Learning Strategies to Remember More in Less Time.

• How Memorize Names, Dates, Game Cards and Useful Info Like a Superhero.

• The Main Secret of Better Focus and Concentration.

• High-Speed Memory Tips.

• A Brain-Enhancing and Memory Improvement Menu.

• An Action Plan for How to Improve Memory in Two Weeks.

• Foreign Language Hacking - The Best Methods to Learn and Speak a New Language.

- The Beginner's Guide to Developing Photographic Memory Skills.

+ BONUS: 21 Memory Improvement Exercises and Techniques

You will see you some real-life examples, case studies that illustrate how people put into practice the points explained, with excellent results. These scenarios will give you a clear idea of how to apply the methods we have talked about in this book. To protect the privacy of the individuals, we have chosen to introduce alternate names.

We invite you to come on this journey to enhance your brainpower. You will discover how exciting it is to develop your memory and increase your concentration. Then, you can truly be the most successful and fulfilled version of yourself.

Read on to find out further about how you can remember more, stress less, and enjoy a meaningful and productive life starting right now!

REFERENCES

https://www.powerofpositivity.com/9-signs-trapped-mind/

https://www.psychologytoday.com/ca/blog/what-mentally-strong-people-dont-do/201602/6-tips-stop-overthinking

https://www.betterhelp.com/advice/personality-disorders/what-is-overthinking-disorder/

https://www.quora.com/What-is-the-difference-between-worry-and-overthinking

https://www.helpguide.org/articles/anxiety/obssessive-compulsive-disorder-ocd.htm/

https://www.helpguide.org/articles/depression/depression-symptoms-and-warning-signs.htm

https://universityhealthnews.com/daily/depression/what-causes-depression/

https://lifehacker.com/what-anxiety-actually-does-to-you-and-what-you-can-do-a-1468128356

https://www.helpguide.org/articles/anxiety/how-to-stop-worrying.htm/

https://www.psychologytoday.com/us/blog/why-we-worry/201206/10-tips-manage-your-worrying

https://www.psychologytoday.com/ca/blog/what-mentally-strong-people-dont-do/201705/how-stop-worrying-about-things-you-cant-change

https://www.huffingtonpost.ca/2013/10/01/stop-worrying-anxiety-cycle_n_4002914.html

https://www.forbes.com/sites/alicegwalton/2017/10/21/a-better-way-to-deal-with-the-negative-thoughts-in-our-heads/#5f45785073e4

https://moodsmith.com/intrusive-thoughts/

https://elysesantilli.com/negative-thoughts/

https://www.powerofpositivity.com/negative-thinking-affects-your-brain/

https://www.brainmdhealth.com/blog/how-to-get-rid-of-harmful-toxins/

https://www.successconsciousness.com/mental-noise.htm

https://www.successconsciousness.com/index_000005.htm

https://blog.mindvalley.com/calm-your-mind-quiet-mental-chatter/

https://upliftconnect.com/how-to-reboot-your-brain/

https://community.uservoice.com/blog/analysis-paralysis-what-it-is-and-how-to-avoid-it/

https://personalexcellence.co/blog/analysis-paralysis/

https://www.lifehack.org/articles/lifestyle/13-tips-to-face-your-fear-and-enjoy-the-ride.html

https://www.apa.org/ptsd-guideline/patients-and-families/exposure-therapy

https://blog.mindvalley.com/the-power-of-positive-thinking/

https://www.briantracy.com/blog/personal-success/positive-attitude-happy-people-positive-thinking/

https://buffer.com/resources/how-to-rewire-your-brains-for-positivity-and-happiness

https://www.positivityblog.com/how-to-quickly-change-a-negative-mood-into-a-positive-one/

https://www.success.com/7-practical-tips-to-achieve-a-positive-mindset/

https://www.sleepfoundation.org/insomnia/what-insomnia

https://www.womenshealthmag.com/health/a19973281/anxiety-sleep/